TO MY BROTHERS IN CHRIST

To My Brothers In Christ
Copyright © 2023 John A. Crawford

All rights reserved.

No part of this publication may be reproduced in a retrieval system, or transmitted in any form or by any means—electronic, mechanical, photocopying, recording, or otherwise—without the prior written permission of the publisher.

Scripture translation credits here.

This manuscript has undergone viable editorial work and proofreading, yet human limitations may have resulted in minor grammatical or syntax-related errors remaining in the finished book. The understanding of the reader is requested in these cases. While precaution has been taken in the preparation of this book, the publisher and author assume no responsibility for errors or omissions, or for damages resulting from the use of the information contained herein.

This book is set in the typeface *Athelas* designed by Veronika Burian and Jose Scaglione.

Paperback ISBN: 979-8-3485-3061-7

A Publication of *Tall Pine Books*
119 E Center Street, Suite B4A | Warsaw, Indiana 46580
www.tallpinebooks.com

| 1 23 23 20 16 02 |

Published in the United States of America

TO MY BROTHERS IN CHRIST

JOHN A. CRAWFORD

To mentor brother in Christ. A father, grandfather prayer warrior and example to all. Champion encourager and great friend. Daryl Gilmore

CONTENTS

Introduction .... *ix*

1. Biggest Man on the Yard 1
2. Build a Strong Foundation 11
3. Remove Distractions 25
4. Legacy 41
5. Leader 53
6. Managing Pressure 65
7. Develop Yourself 79
8. Gate Keepers 91

References *105*
About the Author *107*

INTRODUCTION

Throughout time challenges are encountered in relationships. The challenges can be seen all around us in many areas. The impacts that occur in relationships affect so many others. This often takes place only after so much damage has been done. Not that it is in one community or one ethnic group. It can be seen in every community or ethnic group across the board.

Fault-finding and finger-pointing are not the recipes to getting things resolved. However, there is no quick fix that will make everything better overnight. A person cannot take a pill or cry themselves to sleep, and everything is resolved in the morning. We cannot run some software on the computer and look to the program to fix all the problems. One good place to start would be the WORD of God. Things can take time. We can look at what steps we can take.

Past hurts can turn into roots of bitterness. Bad experiences turn into judgments on others. The innocent can be unaware of the effects of the hurts and bitterness. A person is smiling one minute, and later their arms are crossed, upset.

Many can turn to the advice of friends. The wrong music to calm themselves. Shopping to build self-esteem from depression. They may even turn to habits that will take them down the wrong road, such as clubs, alcohol, drugs, and the wrong company. People can find themselves more upset than before they turned to these different vices. Unfortunately, this process can start at an earlier age than suspected. As it has been said, "Looking for love in all the wrong places."

Now, to answer the question of how to get better relationships with people—turn to the strong foundation. The WORD OF GOD. In the middle of frustration and chaos, it is the last thing many people would think about, but it should be the first. YOU may be surprised to see how the WORD can address your situation. The real results will come when you have a relationship with GOD. Wouldn't it be great to avoid these issues? Prevention would be a great method.

I want to think about this book as if I were sitting down with a group of brothers in Christ and sharing some items that may not be discussed. Thinking on the feedback received from men and women in the past while going through their challenges. Seeing the impact on the children, family, and friends. Everyone cannot sit back and say that every issue and every problem is the man. There are some things we can take a hard and honest look into the details. Some of the things that are brought up may not be comfortable to talk about. Some may be on edge. Some may be offensive. Some things may make you mad. I encourage you to read the book to the end.

You may have to put the letter down because you are upset; however, you can come back to it later and continue. I pray for your God-given desires to come to pass in your life and for you to be able to receive them and keep them in your life. My heart is for you to do better and have better and not be deceived, no matter where you are in life. If you are in a bad state in your life, it can be good. If you are doing good, then become great. Everyone can grow.

Reading the chapters of the letter is best to be able to read with understanding. If you have not received Jesus Christ into your heart, I will encourage you to do so now. If you have in the past and have gotten away from God, I encourage you to recommit your life to Him once again. It would be a great thing for you and give you understanding as you read the content of this letter. There is no judgment here. I'm only helping you to read with understanding and help your spiritual needs to be met.

According to Scripture

> That if you confess with your mouth the Lord Jesus and believe in your heart that God has raised Him from the dead, you will be saved. For with the heart one believes unto righteousness, and with the mouth, confession is made unto salvation. Romans 10:9-10

This can be done in prayer. Invite Jesus Christ into your heart. Believe that He is the son of God and that God has raised Him from the dead. Confess Jesus Christ as Lord.

Say this prayer

> I am a sinner; I need a Savior. I need Jesus. I turn from sin, and I turn to you. I believe in my heart that You raised Jesus from the dead, and I ask Jesus now to come into my heart and be the Lord of my life. I receive Him now as Lord of my life, and I confess with my mouth that Jesus is Lord! Thank you for my salvation! In Jesus' name, Amen.

Now that this has been done, you will better understand what you are about to read.

According to Scripture:

And He said, "To you it has been given to know the mysteries of the kingdom of God, but to the rest it is given in parables, that 'Seeing they may not see, And hearing they may not understand.'" Luke 8:10

Ready. Set. Let's GO!

CHAPTER ONE
BIGGEST MAN ON THE YARD

Who is the Man? This question would be asked to different groups to describe the person that would be on top, in a manner of speaking. Who has the most money? Who has the most women? Who has the most influence? Who has the most connections? The most pull? Who has the juice? Who is the plug? Who has the word on the street? Who has the most inside scoop on what is going on? Who is the go-to guy? Who is the toughest? Who can beat everyone else in every competition? Who is the last man standing? Who has the most toys? WHO IS THE MAN?

God designed THE MAN in His image and His likeness. When this man operates in the dominion that God has created for him to walk out, THE MAN will have whatever is needed to complete his assignment.

> Then God said, "Let Us make man in Our image, according to Our likeness; let them have dominion over the fish of the sea, over the birds of the air, and over the cattle, over all the earth and over every

creeping thing that creeps on the earth." Genesis 1:26

I know I am writing this letter to my brothers in Christ. I know how we are and how we think. I will not waste time. Cut out the mess and get to the point. Make this worth my time reading.

This issue is that men can take a lifetime to try to reach the goal of being known as THE MAN. It is often the wrong goal to reach for the wrong purpose. Do not get me wrong, because there are women that chase after the same things. They want to be seen in a certain way by others. People want to have an image. They want the audacity to proclaim they are a self-made person. This is often done with the wrong heart. It is rooted in pride. This affects the people and the community, especially those looking up to the man. Homes are neglected by a man that is trying to achieve the different things that have been mentioned.

> But he who is greatest among you shall be your servant. Matthew 23:11

A person can seem great because of all the different things they may have achieved. They may be undefeated in their area of expertise. However, that does not make them the greatest above everyone. Even if they may think that they are the greatest. Do not chase the wrong treasure and overlook the treasure that you already have. Everything in life is not about being the biggest or the baddest. That comes with a price that many may not want to pay. They only find this out when it is too late. When they are in that spot, others are trying to take their spot. This would be everyone from the corner block to the corner conference room in the corporation. If the spot is granted to you, be sure that everything is built on integrity. If not, you will see it crumble quicker than you got the position.

Everyone wants to be the top dog. The person that is great for everyone to look up to. They seldom look at the Person that is in that position. We can all study Him and learn from His life.

If you have not known Him yet, let me introduce Him to you—THE MAN Christ Jesus.

> **For there is one God and one Mediator between God and men, <u>the Man Christ</u> Jesus... 1 Timothy 2:5**

He has the most influence of them all. King of Kings and Lord of Lords. He died in the natural over 2,000 years ago and still has influence today because He still lives. He was not weak or, as some would say, a punk. He got beaten by a whip with sharp objects attached to it thirty-nine times. Does that sound like a punk to you? Does that sound like someone who is weak? Not to me. He took it and was still standing.

There are many that are in criminal organizations, gangs, or what have you. They would ask, would this person have the loyalty to die for them? Well, Jesus has already done that and then some. You will never have to question His loyalty to you, but you may have to question your loyalty to Him. He has already died for you. What more could He do? This closes the case on anyone saying He is weak.

WHO IS THE BOSS?

Everyone wants to be a boss, to be the one in charge. They do not realize what comes with being in charge. You are held responsible for anything that occurs when you are in charge. It is all on you. You are the one held accountable. No ducking and hiding. No passing the blame. It is all your decision and your ownership of that decision. NO SHORTCUTS. NO EXCUSES. Again, it is all on you.

If you keep all this in mind, you will make better decisions. It is your name on the line and not anyone else's. You would take more time to think things through before you conclude. You have resources to help you along these lines. Your resources are closer than you think. We will look at this level of responsibility even further.

The BOSS that comes to mind for me would be Jesus. I know it may sound like a cliché. But, He is the KING of KINGS and the LORD of LORDs. He has this title for a reason. He was willing to sacrifice to allow others to succeed. You can tell by the things that He said and the things that He did for others.

> **Greater love has no one than this, than to lay down one's life for his friends. John 15:13**

I'm not saying you die physically here and now for those that you are leading; however, there may be a time that you would give up what you want to do for your own pleasure to help those that you are leading. It is part of being the BOSS.

> **"Father, if it is Your will, take this cup away from Me; nevertheless not My will, but Yours, be done." Luke 22:42**

By looking at this level of responsibility further, we look at what Jesus did in this verse. He was praying for the will of God in this situation. As a leader, we would need to do the same. Before we even start anything, we need to discern the WILL of God first and foremost.

In all your ways acknowledge Him, And He shall direct your paths. Proverbs 3:6

You would acknowledge God by praying to God. This process will come by spending time reading the Bible and talking to God in prayer. Continue to do this on a regular basis. This will develop what we call a prayer life and a relationship with God.

While developing this relationship, you can seek God for the talents and gifts He has given you. What are your abilities? What can you do best with the least amount of effort that would align with His will and purpose for your life? Don't worry or be concerned about what He has for you. It will be something that you like. That is partly why the talent or gift was given to you.

Once you discover your talents and gifts, you can begin to develop them. This may take you to college to develop them. It may be organizations. It may be getting a mentor that operates in the same gift. To be clear. This gift will align with God's Word. God would not give you a talent of sin for you to develop. God would not go against His Word. You need to know what is in God's Word to discern whether your actions align with His Word. For example, you would not have a God-given talent not to get caught selling something illegal. Your gift may be in sales, but you must get another product. I hope that you get my drift. You can learn by helping someone else with what they have taking place currently.

And if you have not been faithful in what is another man's, who will give you what is your own? Luke 16:12

Keep this in mind. You will have to follow before you can lead. It will take time to develop your gifts, talents, and abilities. But it will be well worth the time. You will have a stronger foundation to build your vision. You will learn and develop the skill set along with discipline.

> **A man's gift makes room for him, And brings him before great men. Proverbs 18:16**

After you have developed in a different area, you will find people calling you THE MAN for that area of expertise. You will have experience. You will have a history to show people what you have done. You will have contacts ready to go. You will be the BOSS now. You will be the plug at this point. It will be in a unique way now. You will not be the so-called self-made man. You can now tell everyone what God did for you and through you.

In the process of reading this, I am sure that you are thinking about things right now. I know how we are and how we think. Some of you already have some things in place that you want to get started on developing. You already have something in the works. Word of caution. Get before God to be sure this is what He has for you. Even if it is, you will still want to go to Him. He may have further details and ideas for you to bring to fruition.

As you become a BOSS you will become a plug to other BOSSES. When you align this in scripture. You will be a branch on the vine for Jesus that will bear fruit.

> **"I am the vine; you are the branches. He who abides in Me, and I in him, bears much fruit; for without Me you can do nothing. (John 15:5)"**

As a BOSS, you should look out for your people. It is not all about you. Think about others. You want to make sure they are successful. Make sure they take steps to improve their lives, just as a father looks out for his children. The state of the child will reflect the father. We are not just talking about those that are around us. This would be your family. Your friends. Your neighbors. Your community. Not that this would be done to get an award of some type. It would all be part of building strong communities and strong families. We are MEN!

WHAT EXAMPLE IS BEING SET?

There are times when things are done out of habit. People can become so accustomed to a routine and not even realize what they are doing. Someone may have grown up in an environment accustomed to doing things a certain way. The lifestyle we live and the things we do will have an impact on others. In some environments, some would think that the only way to be successful is to steal, cheat, sell drugs, or be a stripper.

I remember a time when there was a friend of mine from school that I walked home with one day. We were both teenagers. He had an older cousin that was there that day that I met for the first time. His cousin was upset because of an altercation with someone at a high school. He said the conflict went from a strong conversation to an argument. Then from the argument to a weapon being pulled out. Wow. It went from an argument to a weapon being pulled out. They just skipped the physical part. No fist fight but a gun fight. What really caught my attention was that he was having this conversation with his mother. She had no problem with the actions that her son took. They all addressed it like it was a way of life. The actions that are taken are being watched by someone. The actions are making an influence. We have to evaluate what we are doing. Adjustments can be made to align our actions with the Word of God.

Some may think that the only way to be respected is by putting down someone else, hurting someone else, or making someone look bad to make themselves look good. We do not have to operate that way. Think about Jesus. He did not have to get in a sword fight to show strength. He did not have to put someone down to make Himself look good. If anything, Jesus was lifting people up. The man blind from birth, the lady at the well, and even the man at the pool of Bethesda, to name a few. Jesus stated He was the Son of God. He did not have to set Himself out to prove it to anyone. He just stayed on course with what He was called to do. Jesus remained the same and did not change for anyone. Just as Jesus was, we can be the same. We do not have anything to prove.

I know this sounds like a cliché, but Jesus is the example we need to think about. Jesus was popular. However, not everyone liked Him. Jesus stayed on the course assigned to Him, not looking to please people. His focus was to please God. When others have a different agenda, they will work against what God has planned.

> **So all those in the synagogue, when they heard these things, were filled with wrath, and rose up and thrust Him out of the city; and they led Him to the brow of the hill on which their city was built, that they might throw Him down over the cliff. Then passing through the midst of them, He went His way. Luke 4:28-30**

When looking at this, I can see how Jesus had a group of people trying to push Him not only into a corner but off a cliff. Talk about a serious situation. Yet, Jesus still passed through them. I would not imagine Jesus saying excuse me as He passed through the group. I would not have even expected Him to be nice about it and smile at the group. Let me ask you a question. Does this sound like someone that is weak? Not so.

He did not have a problem setting this straight and standing up for what was right in His Father's eyes. People were being cheated in the temple regarding the doves they brought to the temple for an offering. They were forced to pay more money and were told that what they brought was unacceptable. Jesus called them out on it.

> **So they came to Jerusalem. Then Jesus went into the temple and began to drive out those who bought and sold in the temple, and overturned the tables of the money changers and the seats of those who sold doves. And He would not allow anyone to carry wares through the temple. Then He taught, saying to them, "Is it not written, 'My house shall be called a house of prayer for all nations'? But you have made it a 'den of thieves.'" Mark 11:15-17**

You can see why they hated Him because He called them out for their actions. These are just a few examples of Jesus doing what is right even when it was not liked by those that were in His path.

WRAP UP:

It is not about who is the biggest or the baddest. There will always be someone that is bigger or better than you are. You may not have met them up until this point. A person's body will not stay in the same condition their entire life. The one that will outlast us all is Jesus. He has given you the opportunity to have everlasting life. I would encourage you to invite Jesus into your heart and into your life. Don't just think about Him when you are in trouble or faced with a challenge. He is the big one in the yard, and He is recruiting others that will follow His example. If you are challenged with seeing Jesus as the biggest or the most important, look at what God had to say about Him and where God placed Him.

> **Which He worked in Christ when He raised Him from the dead and seated Him at His right hand in the heavenly places far above all principality and power and might and dominion, and every name that is named, not only in this age but also in that which is to come. And He put all things under His feet, and gave Him to be head over all things to the church, which is His body, the fullness of Him who fills all in all. Ephesians 1:20-23**

There is a lot that can be accomplished by inviting God to help us in all that we are doing. It can be personally or in the community helping others. To do this, we must keep our relationship with God active. This involves reading the Bible and getting to know Him better. We can all work to do better in this area. Another thing you can do is go to church. This will put you among others of the same mind. You will be able to learn and help others. Finally, you must cultivate a prayer life, meaning you take the time to pray on a regular basis. It is just like talking to a close friend who does not tell everyone else all your business. I pray this is not getting too preachy but that it is helpful to you.

CHAPTER 2
BUILD A STRONG FOUNDATION

> Therefore whoever hears these sayings of Mine, and does them, I will liken him to a wise man who built his house on the rock. Matthew 7:24

When building anything you want to be successful, it should be strong, long-lasting, durable, tough, and to be able to weather the storm. In order to accomplish this, consider the foundation. Again, we are thinking about being successful. How successful do you want to be? A little success? An enormous success? This would help to determine how strong you would need to build your foundation. The higher you want a building to be would require a deeper foundation to support the structure.

It is an interesting contrast between the foundation of a building and the foundation of a person's life. Consider the material and support systems needed to maintain the foundation. What is it made of? What is the grass root of the items? Is it structured in a way that will last? Will it be made of mortar, stone, brick, or concrete? Will there be wood or steel to provide the extra support for the house and foundation? There are a lot of questions that can come up before building this house. But just as God's Word instructs us to count the cost, we also need to consider the cost of constructing the house. The foundation will be essential to keeping the house together.

> **For which of you, intending to build a tower, does not sit down first and count the cost, whether he has enough to finish it— lest, after he has laid the foundation, and is not able to finish, all who see it begin to mock him...**
> **Luke 14:28-29**

Once the cost and the commitment are enough to cover the foundation being constructed, the techniques to construct the foundation must be considered. This foundation will need to keep that moisture and mold out of the house. It will help insulate the home and also what holds the house together. Everything under the house will still need to remain dry. This is a significant factor in keeping the foundation in place, which will stop the earth from moving the house. You need a solid foundation. The movement will impact the entire house, and as you can see, the foundation holds the house together. If someone is considering committing their lives to Jesus Christ, they must first consider the cost. This is crucial because one can have an excellent start only to quit when things get hard, or they face challenges. Anyone can start something. Things can sound good or even look good; however, it takes character to continue when things go wrong and times are hard. Consider the cost ahead of time. Know well ahead of what you are committing to. When you make a good, sound decision ahead of time, it is easier to know the course of action to take. When issues arise, you will remember your commitment. Remembering the commitment will help you to stay on track.

"Therefore whoever hears these sayings of Mine, and does them, I will liken him to a wise man who built his house on the rock: and the rain descended, the floods came, and the winds blew and beat on that house; and it did not fall, for it was founded on the rock. But everyone who hears these sayings of Mine, and does not do them, will be like a foolish man who built his house on the sand: and the rain descended, the floods came, and the winds blew and beat on that house; and it fell. And great was its fall." Matthew 7:24-26

EAGLE'S MOUNTAINS

Just as Jesus trusted the Father, seeing the birds doing the same is impressive. It just occurs to them naturally. It is not planned. When thinking about the Alaskan bald eagle, they do many things to be prepared. A bird would weigh less than a human being; however, the eagle's nest would be on a structure or, shall we say, a foundation that could hold just over a thousand pounds. The nest is generally in a place that is higher than the average bird. They build their nest on cliffs, rock promontories, and maybe some old dead trees. Notice that they will be sure that the foundation will hold just over a thousand pounds. The nest that they build would typically be four to six feet in diameter. All of this comes to the eagle naturally. The eagle has a plan and makes the preparations needed to bring it all to pass. The eagle will consider the foundation, the materials, and even the nest's location. If a bird has this intelligence in building a house in nature, we can have more intelligence in building our natural and spiritual house. When thinking about the materials of a natural foundation, who do we allow in our lives to build our spiritual foundation? What groups are we taking part in? Are there different influences we would allow in our lives or families? You are the gatekeeper with all that God has entrusted you to steward. What environment will you create for you and your family to live in?

> Look at the birds of the air, for they neither sow nor reap nor gather into barns; yet your heavenly Father feeds them. Are you not of more value than they? Which of you by worrying can add one cubit to his stature? Matthew 6:26-27

Jesus said to build on a strong foundation.

BUILD YOUR HOUSE ON THE ROCK

> According to the grace of God, which was given to me, as a wise master builder I have laid the foundation, and another builds on it. But let each one take heed how he builds on it. For no other foundation can anyone lay than that which is laid, which is Jesus Christ. Now if anyone builds on this foundation with gold, silver, precious stones, wood, hay, straw, each one's work will become clear; for the Day will declare it, because it will be revealed by fire; and the fire will test each one's work, of what sort it is. If anyone's work which he has built on it endures, he will receive a reward. If anyone's work is burned, he will suffer loss; but he himself will be saved, yet so as through fire. 1 Corinthians 3:10-15

YOUR FOUNDATION

Have the house that FAITH built. Let your house be built on the Word of God. Just as there are varied materials in a house's foundation, faith and God's Word are strong, long-lasting foundations.

Develop your relationship with God just as you would with a natural relationship. In a natural relationship, you would spend time with the person. You would get to know them. Find out their likes and dislikes. The more you spend time with the person, the better you get to know them and the closer you become. You will always have them on your mind. You will repeat what the person says and recall what they have done. You would remember the outcomes of what they have done, and you would tell others and share all the experiences that took place. Likewise, you can take the time to develop a relationship with God. It does not have to be the business of anyone else, but this can be a legacy you can leave to your children and others whose lives you influence.

A man who has friends must himself be friendly, But there is a friend who sticks closer than a brother. Proverbs 18:24

Operate in the same way when it comes to God. Times can be challenging. There may have been people you have trusted in the past that have disappointed you. You will not have that issue when it comes to God. People may have pretended to be what they are not or proclaimed to be more than what they are. But God is not like that. He does not make you think He is something He is not. Unfortunately, people will often do that or misrepresent God. It may seem that God is not what you think He is at times; however, you will need to get to know Him better. He does not change. The key is that you cannot just stop at one place in your life and think, "Is that it? I thought there was more." You must continue in His word to know Him better. As you continue in God's Word, more truth will be revealed. Your relationship will grow stronger. You will find yourself moving forward without fear.

> Then Jesus said to those Jews who believed Him, "If you abide in My word, you are My disciples indeed." John 8:31

> Jesus Christ is the same yesterday, today, and forever. Hebrews 13:8

> Now when they saw the boldness of Peter and John, and perceived that they were uneducated and untrained men, they marveled. And they realized that they had been with Jesus. Acts 4:13

Jesus had a strong relationship with His Father. You can see this in the things that took place in His life. Jesus made mention of His Father repeatedly. He spent time with His Father regularly. We can take that as an example. By having this strong relationship with the Father, He always knew what to do and when to execute what was to be done. Can you just imagine how we can do the same? Jesus did not understand all of the instructions that the Father gave Him. He was in a position where he had to put His trust in the Father. Again, we can do the same. It may seem impossible, but all things are possible with God. Go ahead and reach for that dream, regardless of how hard it may seem. Just as it occurred with Peter and John, the same can happen with you. You will have boldness as you trust what God has said. You will begin to build a history of doing the same. Remember Jesus as a human example of all that we can do. Believe it or not, we can do even greater.

> Most assuredly, I say to you, he who believes in Me, the works that I do he will do also; and greater works than these he will do, because I go to My Father. John 14:12

The things that you do today will affect your tomorrow. The actions that you take will not only affect you today. They will affect you, your family, your friends, and others that you encounter. This will be important for the foundation that is built. Many are so short-sighted. They do not think long-term. They think so often of instant microwave gratification. The devil will never show you all the consequences on the other side. It's been said, "Sin will take you farther than you want to go, keep you longer than you want to stay, and cost you more than you want to pay." It sounds good and looks good initially but will affect you in the long run. This will have a negative impact on your foundation. You can be in a place to lead others and find it to be a challenge when they always bring up the past. People can tend to dwell on all of the wrong things and forget all the good you have done. This is natural for people. I'm just bringing this up for you to have in mind. There can be a soccer game for the World Cup, and the goalie can miss the ball just one time. The news telecast will highlight it and play it again and again. It will be all the talk on Sports Center. Everyone forgets all the times that the person stopped all the balls that got the team in the successful position that they are in.

Likewise, people will always talk about the negative and disregard the good you have done. Don't go the negative route out of your emotions. It is not worth it in the long run. You are able to overcome this and have control. You can have peace in a stressful situation. Keep yourself around the right company. This is important for you to maintain. You are the rock. You are the main foundation that keeps the house together. Unfortunately, that can be why the man is constantly under attack. So many are against the family. Many want to redefine the family. Many don't want you to succeed. The man can be reflected in a negative manner in so many different places that you look. In the news, television programs, films, social media, and everywhere you look. The man can be labeled negatively. A man can feel that it is always him against the world. Just remember that God will never leave you or forsake you. If you find no one in your corner, remember that He will always be there. Even if everyone is against you, He will always be there.

> **Let your conversation be without covetousness; and be content with such things as ye have: for he hath said, I will never leave thee, nor forsake thee. Hebrews 13:5**

> **So Jesus answered and said to them, "Have faith in God. For assuredly, I say to you, whoever says to this mountain, 'Be removed and be cast into the sea,' and does not doubt in his heart, but believes that those things he says will be done, he will have whatever he says. Mark 11:22-23**

Another thing that can impact your foundation can be temptations. The temptations can come to you in different forms. Not every temptation can be in the form of sin. Something can appear to be more money in a quick amount of time. Something can look like it is low in price, but it might cost you so much more in repairs in the long run. Other things can be of a sinful nature. Someone can try to talk you into taking advantage of somebody and try to rip them off. Temptation can come for you to cheat. You must stand strong and resist these things. Your foundation cannot be impacted. The timing that these things can occur can be amazing. It is not by coincidence. It is by the devil's design. Do not take the bait. Stand strong. Jesus had to face the same challenges. He set the example for us all to stand strong. We can be the same example to others.

Then was Jesus led up of the Spirit into the wilderness to be tempted of the devil. And when he had fasted forty days and forty nights, he was afterward an hungred. And when the tempter came to him, he said, If thou be the Son of God, command that these stones be made bread. But he answered and said, It is written, Man shall not live by bread alone, but by every word that proceedeth out of the mouth of God. Then the devil taketh him up into the holy city, and setteth him on a pinnacle of the temple, And saith unto him, If thou be the Son of God, cast thyself down: for it is written, He shall give his angels charge concerning thee: and in their hands they shall bear thee up, lest at any time thou dash thy foot against a stone. Jesus said unto him, It is written again, Thou shalt not tempt the Lord thy God. Again, the devil taketh him up into an exceeding high mountain, and sheweth him all the kingdoms of the world, and the glory of them; And saith unto him, All these things will I give thee, if thou wilt fall down and worship me. Then saith Jesus unto him, Get thee hence, Satan: for it is written, Thou shalt worship the Lord thy God, and him only shalt thou serve. Then the devil leaveth him, and, behold, angels came and ministered unto him. Mark 4:1-11

Jesus was tempted to prove Himself. He had nothing to prove. He was offered the kingdoms of the world and the glory of them. Jesus still stood strong. He spoke to all of the temptations and said, "It is written." He stayed on His course and did not compromise. If He had changed, it would have negatively impacted us all. When you are the leader, the man, and the head, your decisions will impact others. Have a relationship with God. Seek His face. He will always be there to help you make the right choices.

> **Jesus said to him, "If you can believe, all things are possible to him who believes. Mark 9:23**

EVALUATE YOUR FOUNDATION

To have the proper maintenance with a house, you would have a regular routine check of different things to be sure that everything is in proper working order. It is recommended that the foundation be inspected at least once a year. This will help you see if anything needs to be done. See if there is any movement or anything that would need to be addressed. In the same fashion, you will need to have a routine check on your foundation. See if some things need to be addressed. This process is more common than you think. When someone is working at a job, they get a yearly performance review. It is also recommended that everyone get a physical once a year. So, if these are so common and easy to understand, why not do the same for our lives and families? This would not only make things better for you, but it will help others that are involved. This will help you to maintain focus.

1. WHAT COMPANY ARE YOU KEEPING?

You will need to evaluate the friendships, associations, memberships, social groups, and those that you are hanging around. You need to determine the health of these relationships. Make the adjustments that need to be made. As a man, it would be better to put emotions aside and make tough decisions. Are there people that are just around to ask for money? Are there people that are a bad influence? Is there a woman around in areas of your life that is not appropriate? Are there people in your life that constantly use you? Have the right people in your life. MAKE THE ADJUSTMENTS THAT ARE NEEDED.

> As iron sharpens iron, So a man sharpens the countenance of his friend. Proverbs 27:17

2. WHAT ARE YOU WATCHING?

There may be things on different media platforms such as TV, social media, newspapers, magazines, podcasts, movies, radio broadcasts, and other forms of media. By being inundated with all these things, you can be impacted in a very subtle way. You may not even realize the impact that they have on you. You will say or believe something one day and say and believe something else on another day. If you think I am wrong in stating this, I will challenge you to listen to sports fans talk about sports. If you listen to them long enough and pay close attention, you will find some things are not consistent. They listen to something else and change their opinion. This point is especially important because if that can happen in a sports conversation, imagine the impact if you get off track with what the Bible says. We all must allow the Bible (Word of God) to guide us. It will help us stay on track. MAKE THE ADJUSTMENTS THAT ARE NEEDED.

3. WHAT ARE YOU DOING REGARDING YOUR HEALTH?

I mentioned earlier about getting a yearly physical. It would be best to get checked out once a year. Be able to address things earlier on and not be shocked when something happens. The women in your life will be concerned if this is being neglected. They would be the right women in your life that are there for the right reasons. It can be a mother, aunt, teacher, or others. It is a way they are telling you that they love you. MAKE THE ADJUSTMENTS THAT ARE NEEDED.

4. WHAT ARE YOU DOING WITH YOUR FINANCES?

Everyone can talk about all the money they have and all the things that they have. Not many are thinking about the future. Have investments and make moves for your future. Your family will wonder how this is being handled. As a single person, if you meet a young lady, she and her family will want to know your plans. As a married man, your wife would be concerned about this area. Have a plan. She will need to be on board with that plan. You need God's guidance on how to manage your finances. Surround yourself with people you can trust in this area. Be sure they have a track record and have success in their own finances. MAKE THE ADJUSTMENTS THAT ARE NEEDED.

5. HOW ARE THINGS WITH THE FAMILY?

As the leader, you will need to see the things taking place with your family. If you are single, you will need to keep a watch on everything. Just as a coach would be able to see more on the bench than the player in the game, you will need to be able to see what is occurring with the family, friends, and other relationships. It can seem hard, but this is possible with the help of God. As you know, God sees and hears everything. God would greatly help in this area as you are seeking Him. Who do I need to spend time with? Who needs more attention in this area? Who needs support with art, math, driving, etc.? MAKE THE ADJUSTMENTS THAT ARE NEEDED.

6. WHAT ARE YOU DOING TO DEVELOP SPIRITUALLY?

At a minimum, I would say at least read the Bible primarily. This is a sure way to firm up your foundation. As a leader, you will have this firm foundation to stand on in every situation. In order to develop your foundation, it is essential to attend church regularly. Go to a church that is teaching and preaching according to the Bible (Word of God). This will put you around others that have successfully gone through the same challenges that you may have. This would put you in a position to learn and grow. Have a time that you talk to and pray to God on a regular basis. Have a prayer life. When you are asked what you are going to do, God can be your plug that was mentioned earlier. God can provide you with answers as you seek Him. MAKE THE ADJUSTMENTS THAT ARE NEEDED.

7. WHAT ARE YOU DOING TO DEVELOP PROFESSIONALLY?

If you have a lot of time and no money, you can use the time to your advantage. Look to see what programs are available. There are companies that need help. The condition is that you will need to be willing to work. Some colleges even offer free online courses. Take advantage of that. If you volunteer to help someone, you can develop a skill and get educated that way. Not only will you pick up a skill, but you will also have work experience. There are public libraries where you can go and read books for free. Always be advancing. MAKE THE ADJUSTMENTS THAT ARE NEEDED.

WRAP UP

Building a strong foundation will be very important for you because you will be the strong foundation that others rely on. Just as a house's foundation is the strong force that holds a family together, you will be the strong foundation that holds the family together. You will want to be a foundation that others can trust and come to where there will be truth and love. When you are on the right foundation, you will be a safe place that the family and their friends can come to and not be deceived. Everything may not always be bright and sunny, but you will want to keep your integrity in this position. Many do not want the family unit to remain and constantly try to attack the family. The foundation must be firm to keep the family/community intact. We must build our house on the Rock to weather the storms of life.

CHAPTER 3
REMOVE DISTRACTIONS

When I was a child, I spoke as a child, I understood as a child, I thought as a child; but when I became a man, I put away childish things. 1 Corinthians 13:11

As men, there are some childish things we need to put away. We must put them away for us to be as effective as God desires us to be. They might be mental, emotional, or physical. Whatever the case, we need to put them away. Wrong relationships, thoughts, and bad habits can be put away with the right discipline. We must remove distractions.

God has a destiny for our lives. There are so many things He wants us to fulfill in His destiny for us. We cannot fulfill that destiny if we do not have a relationship with Him. That is not to say things will come easy because you set out to do them. If you go along with the crowd, you will get the results of the crowd. If you strive to be like everyone else and do everything they do, how can you find your uniqueness? If everyone is the same, they are all to solve the same problems. They are all at the same place in life.

You were not created to be the same as everyone else. You were created for a purpose. You cannot be deceived into being just like everyone else. That would be a distraction. In order to master this, you will need to remove distractions. You are unique, and God has something specific for you.

> **I will praise You, for I am fearfully and wonderfully made; Marvelous are Your works, And that my soul knows very well. Psalm 139:14**

People will always make a special effort to stand out. They will have the same basic style but have a little something that is different. They will say things like, " Nobody has these shoes." Something will be different about their car from everyone else, but they will have the same basic car. So many are ready to stand out to get the attention of others. Are you ready to come out from among them?

> **Therefore "Come out from among them And be separate, says the Lord. Do not touch what is unclean, And I will receive you. 2 Corinthians 6:17**

There may be a time when you have to stand alone. Everyone will not congratulate you for what you are doing. I encourage you to stay focused on the plan and purpose for your life. You will be more effective in staying focused by removing distractions from your life. One of the most challenging things about being distracted is being in a situation where you do not realize you are being distracted. When a person is in this state, they are not paying attention. A few examples would be a person getting bumped and their wallet being taken from their pocket or the way a man is with a woman. Or a con artist performing their con or manipulation to get things from you. As the saying goes, "When God wants to bless you, He will put someone in your life. If the devil wants to bring you harm to what God has for you, he will send someone into your life." You will definitely need to know the difference between the two. A relationship with God and a regular prayer life will tremendously help in this area to give you a stronger discernment.

I remember a time when a church function was taking place. There was an outreach that was to take place for college students. I could relate to them very well. In college, I went with some friends to church occasionally. It's funny how you always remember the food you ate during these times. The outreach was set up to give the college students a meal, free time, and some time for the message to be preached. Everything was free for the college students. I was on a college campus one day handing out flyers. I had to deal with the distinct rules that the administration had laid out. They could not be biased in any way. They told me the areas where I could place the flyers for the students. I went to the area and saw all the different events that were to take place at the same time of the event at the church. The night clubs were having college night events. Other clubs had all the girls on their flyers to entice people to come to their clubs. I understood what that was all about. The club promoters wanted to make money. Clearly, the images and the activities on those flyers were a distraction. I have been there, but I have grown wiser over time. It was interesting to see how the night turned out. There was a long line of students at the church. Most of them were females. I was thinking about the guys. They must have gone to the clubs and thought what we had to offer was boring. They may not have been interested at the moment.

What the guys were looking at and getting involved with was short-term. The females that were in the line had long-term goals in mind. You could tell by where they chose to come. You could tell by how they were dressed. It was much different from a crowd of people talking about the next party, the people they know, and who is sexually active. Now compare that to a crowd asking what your major is or if you have any thoughts about what you will do after school. They see how your interest aligns with your major. They don't just know who you hang around with but what your family is like. People like that can hold you more accountable to attain your dreams. Not that they will stay on you or even push you. You can be motivated to pursue your dreams by watching them pursue their dreams. I wonder if the guys were at the club and met the person that the devil was putting in their life to trip them up and missed out on the possibility of the person that God would have tried to place in their life. Things can happen that fast if you are not paying attention. Do not take the bait.

There can be opposition against you and God's plan for your life. There can be people that hate you and everything that you stand for. Do it anyway. It is not just for you. Go against the opposition anyway. If God is for you, who can be against you? Sometimes, people will not like what you are doing, and people will directly hate what you are doing and make plans to go against what you are doing. You don't have to tell everyone everything about what God has for you or the things that God has for you to do. Do not cast your pearls before swine.

> **Do not give what is holy to the dogs; nor cast your pearls before swine, lest they trample them under their feet, and turn and tear you in pieces. Matthew 7:6**

Now that you see what the swine will do, you must know why you do not need to put your pearls before the swine. You do not have to tell everyone all of your business. They do not need to know all your ideas, thoughts, or plans for the future. Not everyone has your best interests at heart. The following is one example of how a good work was brought to the attention of the wrong people.

NEHEMIAH'S OPPOSITION TO BUILDING THE WALL

There is a biblical account of a cupbearer named Nehemiah, who was the servant of King Artaxerxes. He requested to go to the city of Judah, the city of his fathers' tombs, to rebuild. The permission was granted. The king provided people and resources for the good work that he set out to do. Unfortunately, others found out what he was doing. He was laughed at and despised at first. Then people plotted against him out of hatred for what he was doing.

(LAUGHED AND DESPISED)

> Then I said to them, "You see the distress that we are in, how Jerusalem lies waste, and its gates are burned with fire. Come and let us build the wall of Jerusalem, that we may no longer be a reproach." And I told them of the hand of my God which had been good upon me, and also of the king's words that he had spoken to me. So, they said, "Let us rise up and build." Then they set their hands to this good work. But when Sanballat the Horonite, Tobiah the Ammonite official, and Geshem the Arab heard of it, they laughed at us and despised us, and said, "What is this thing that you are doing? Will you rebel against the king?" So I answered them, and said to them, "The God of heaven Himself will prosper us; therefore we His servants will arise and build, but you have no heritage or right or memorial in Jerusalem." Nehemiah 2:17-20

(PLOTTED AGAINST)

> Now it happened, when Sanballat, Tobiah, the Arabs, the Ammonites, and the Ashdodites heard that the walls of Jerusalem were being restored and the gaps were beginning to be closed, that they became very angry, and all of them conspired together to come and attack Jerusalem and create confusion. Nevertheless we made our prayer to our God, and because of them we set a watch against them day and night. Nehemiah 4:7-9

There was a lot that Nehemiah encountered when performing this good work that God placed in his heart for him to do. There were many obstacles in his way. Sometimes, the workers constructed with one hand and had a weapon in the other. They were prepared for an attack if it came down to a fight. There were other attempts of manipulation to try to deceive him and stop him from what he was doing. Regardless of the opposition, Nehemiah continued to stay focused.

(THE WORK IS COMPLETED)

> So the wall was finished on the twenty-fifth day of Elul, in fifty-two days. And it happened, when all our enemies heard of it, and all the nations around us saw these things, that they were very disheartened in their own eyes; for they perceived that this work was done by our God. Nehemiah 6:15-16

People can plot and scheme and not even realize they are deliberately going against God's plan. They are bringing harm to themselves with selfish ambitions, jealousy, or vindictiveness. Just because they operate in the wrong spirit does not mean they must take you off course. Just as Nehemiah continued to move forward and stay consistent with his God-given vision, we all can do the same. If you feel stuck in a position where you cannot do anything but believe, then do that! Believe!

> **Confess your trespasses to one another, and pray for one another, that you may be healed. The effective, fervent prayer of a righteous man avails much. James 5:16**

Nehemiah believed, and we can see what he accomplished. Do not give up on what God has given to you. Have a purpose. Walk in the Spirit rather than fulfill the lust of the flesh.

WALKING IN THE SPIRIT

> **I say then: Walk in the Spirit, and you shall not fulfill the lust of the flesh. Galatians 5:16**

Focusing on what God has for you to do will prevent you from wasting time and money because everything you do will be working toward what He has set out for you to do. Do not be moved by what the media is telling you. Study things out. Don't let fear grip you. Find out the truth.

It is amazing how so many people can remember everything with celebrity gossip, stats for athletes, and teams winning records for years, but they cannot recite one Bible verse to help them in their current situation. The lines for a new pair of sneakers are out the door, and the library is empty. The now-hiring lines are empty, but the nightclubs and entertainment shows are full. See how people can be distracted by what is not important. Not to say that wholesome recreational things are unimportant, but people must have the right priorities. Things are not going to occur by happenstance.

Other cultures attend school all year long. Some are forced to serve in the military for two years when they finish high school. Men and women. Some cultures force citizens to take certain courses in high school and college. It would be difficult to compete in the marketplace while being in line for the next shoe that came out. Why not own the company that manufactures the shoes? If the player's stats and jersey number can be remembered, why is the person not an agent or somehow making money off their knowledge about the topic? If this is not helping you in any way, remove it quickly. It is a distraction.

Often, we look at what everyone else has that we do not have. I did not realize that we were being set up for something better. We were in an apartment but not in a bad state. I saw others who got a new car every year. They had cable, and we did not. They had the latest fashion and name brands. We did not. The time came, and we got a house. The others were still in an apartment. They still got new cars and had cable. We still did not have cable or other things, but they came in time. And over time, I saw some of the others remain in the same situation. You have to remove the distraction when others seem to have it all, and you do not. You do not know how they got what they got. My dad made sacrifices to allow the family to get to the next level. I remember him taking me with him to pick up my mom from work. I would be outside riding my big wheel in the neighborhood. He would pick me up and put the big wheel in the back, and off we would go to get my mom. That was a time when the family only had one car. My mom rode the bus to work while my dad drove to his job, which was far from where we lived. Many of my friends' mothers worked at a curtain factory behind us. They did not commute to the job day by day. They were close to home.

There were times when layoffs would occur. I was too young and little to understand what was taking place. My older brother and sister would tell me how things were at those times. They told me my father would be out of work, but some things did not change. Every Friday, we had a special dinner as a family. This was not one of the things that my father sacrificed. We always got that no matter what was happening. I was worried when I saw my dad get laid off as a young teenager. When I saw he was not concerned about it, I stopped worrying. He may not have been in church much at that time in his life, but you could see his faith. My siblings would laugh at the fact that there were times when my dad was laid off and was not looking for one at the time, but the phone would be ringing for him with work. How blessed we were at that time. I am sure others may not have been as fortunate. This became important to my siblings and me as we became adults. When faced with situations, we always have times like this to reflect on to help us move forward. Do not let situations distract you. There is still more out there that can be accomplished. Over time I did learn that God is our source. Regardless of what is going on around you. Regardless of how things may look. God is my source.

Not everyone remained in the same neighborhood. Many moved out and moved on as time went on. That generation was more than willing to work to get what they wanted. The families did not have the direction that is available to us today. When they got tired of a situation, they focused more on what they wanted and where they wanted to be. Some advanced in their careers, started businesses, and did other endeavors. There was one daughter that I heard about that worked to put her parents in a house. After she bought a house for them to live in, she purchased a house for herself. I have so much respect for her doing that for her parents. She did not have to be a millionaire or some successful actress to do this for her parents. She was focused and did it with a regular job.

THINGS CAN BE SO SUBTLE

I had a friend that was living with me for a short time. I was helping him out with his current situation. He had a car that was really customized. It was a very loud purple color paint job. The paint looked new. It had custom reams with custom seats with a white and purple interior to match. The two front seats had small televisions in the back of the headrest. This car could be seen from a distance. The car got a lot of attention. The children in the neighborhood kept staring at the car while it sat in my driveway.

One Saturday afternoon, I was sitting out on my porch. It was a nice spring day, so everyone was out and about. I had a function at the church that I was to volunteer for in a few hours. As I was sitting there on my porch, there seemed to be so many women that were driving by in such a short amount of time. They would look at the car and look at me. They would look at the car and look at me. The feeling made a single man want to stay out on the porch a little longer, but I knew that I had somewhere to be. I know things like this make you feel that you are missing something, but often being where you are supposed to be can keep you out of a lot of trouble. I always thought about King David not being on the battle lines where he should have been, but he was watching Bathsheba take a bath on the rooftop. I left and went to the function where I was to volunteer to work.

The function went well. However, God began sharing some things with me when I got home. He was like, "Okay, Mr. Big Shot. Did you think about all the ladies that were driving by? Did you notice what they were attracted to? Did you take a close look at them? What were they driving? Where were they coming from or going to?" Things began to make more sense. The ladies driving by were not living the lifestyle that I was living. You could tell from how they dressed and even the music they played. If I would just focus on what I needed to be focused on, the right person would have come into place. I needed to get away from those distractions. It was God's way of saying, "You did not miss anything." It is funny as I think about this now because I do not recall that many women driving through the neighborhood since that day. Oh, how a distraction can throw you off track if you allow it.

David had a major distraction in Bathsheba when he was watching her take a bath from his balcony. This was a time that the leader would lead the charge for the battle; however, the king was not in the battle. He stayed back. He had a distraction that caused him to be involved with a married woman. It cost him eventually.

SIN COMMITTED

Then it happened one evening that David arose from his bed and walked on the roof of the king's house. And from the roof he saw a woman bathing, and the woman was very beautiful to behold. So David sent and inquired about the woman. And someone said, "Is this not Bathsheba, the daughter of Eliam, the wife of Uriah the Hittite?" Then David sent messengers, and took her; and she came to him, and he lay with her, for she was cleansed from her impurity; and she returned to her house. And the woman conceived; so she sent and told David, and said, "I am with child." 2 Samuel 11:2-5

The woman Bathsheba was the wife of one of his soldiers. He tried different things to try to cover up the wrong that he did. Regardless of what you do, good or bad, it comes back. We must make the right decisions and not let the lust of the flesh or the pride of life consume us or take us off the track that God has for us.

> **Do not be deceived, God is not mocked; for whatever a man sows, that he will also reap. Galatians 6:7**

(EFFECT OF THE SIN COMMITTED)

> "I gave you your master's house and your master's wives into your keeping and gave you the house of Israel and Judah. And if that had been too little, I also would have given you much more! Why have you despised the commandment of the Lord, to do evil in His sight? You have killed Uriah the Hittite with the sword; you have taken his wife to be your wife, and have killed him with the sword of the people of Ammon. Now therefore, the sword shall never depart from your house, because you have despised Me, and have taken the wife of Uriah the Hittite to be your wife." Thus says the Lord: "Behold, I will raise up adversity against you from your own house; and I will take your wives before your eyes and give them to your neighbor, and he shall lie with your wives in the sight of this sun. For you did it secretly, but I will do this thing before all Israel, before the sun." 2 Samuel 12:8-12

SLEEPING AROUND

In society today, people are very sexually active. It is portrayed as such a casual thing because everyone is doing it. It seems like everyone is participating. Just because everyone else is doing this does not mean you have to participate. Just because you have sex with someone or even with many partners, it does not make you a woman. It does not mean that you are grown. This is not an action that should be taken outside of marriage.

> Now the works of the flesh are evident, which are: adultery, fornication, uncleanness, lewdness.. Galatians 5:19

The movies you watch, and the social media you read, can make it look like this is normal, that it is okay to have this lifestyle. It can look fun and be portrayed as if you are missing out on something. Two people in a movie would have a scene where they would go into a room alone. Once the sexual activity has been completed, one person smokes a cigarette who has never smoked before, as if it causes them to become cool, and you should try it sometime. There is more to this than what meets your eyes. There is more that has been transferred than just a sexual encounter.

The interesting thing about it is that the different forms of media do not show you the bad side. The consequences of the actions can come in unusual ways. Things change after sex is involved. They will not be as they were before. Sexual diseases can be transferred to you. Unplanned pregnancies can occur. Even if you are using protection, there are no guarantees. There are diseases that you can get that there is no cure for. I do not mind missing out on these things with the so-called fun that they are having.

The lie that is being told is that you want to hook up with someone while they are interested, like having sex with them will be something that will keep them around. If the person leaves over sex, what kind of person are you with anyway? There is no need to whet an appetite for something that you should not be doing. Do not whet your appetite and cause a desire for something that needs to go unfulfilled. Other lies tell you to evaluate the waters, see how well the person performs, and know what you are getting before you commit. These lies can cause you to commit to the wrong person, or even worse, can cause you to miss out on the right person that God has for you. If you want something different, you must avoid these lies and do something different.

> **Flee sexual immorality. Every sin that a man does is outside the body, but he who commits sexual immorality sins against his own body. 1 Corinthians 6:18**

I remember a few of the part-time jobs that I had as a teenager. The environments I was in and some of the people I worked with may be alarming to many. Dirty jokes were told. Many sexual references were made. You would have thought the women were offended by the things that were said by others, but they were laughing right with the people telling the dirty jokes. The guys would talk big and say big things when they were around all the fellows. Whenever they would get with me one on one, they would all say nearly the same thing. It would all be along the same lines. The statements would be something like, "Hey. I do not regret having my kids, but I wish I had waited until I was in a better position to take care of them. It would be best for you to wait." Yes, they talked trash all the time, but they took care of their children. I remember one of them had a child that was older than I was at the time. Even though I was not part of everything that they talked about, they were telling me not to do things in the way that they had done in the past. It does not take a lot to come out from among them. I do remember one of them confronting me one night. He was one of the ring leaders of the dirty jokes. Just as he was big and bad enough to tell dirty jokes, he was just as big, just as bad, and just as bold to look at me eye to eye. He told me, "KEEP IT IN YOUR PANTS!" That advice would go right in line with God's Word. That statement came from the right heart.

> Therefore "Come out from among them And be separate, says the Lord. Do not touch what is unclean, And I will receive you." 2 Corinthians 2:17

The Word of God helps us by providing guidelines to keep us out of the dangers that the lifestyle can bring. In other words, we can "Come Out from Among Them." Keeping yourself for marriage would be something that would always be a help in the long term. Keeping yourself in the marriage is even better. We cannot take that part out of the evaluation as many people often do. This may be frowned upon by many, but if the person frowns on what kind of person you are, they are not right for you anyway. If the person cannot respect that, then they will not have respect for you in other aspects of the relationship. Keep that in mind. If you want a person with all this experience, wouldn't that mean the person has been with many people before you? What would that person bring to you? What spirits, diseases, and emotional baggage is coming with the package? Has the person addressed any of these issues? All these elements, along with others, are what you could be inviting into you and around you, to be direct about it.

WRAP UP

As men, we can not allow things to trip us up. Being the head can put you in front of a lot of opposition. There will be temptations and different things that can come against the man. Stay strong and understand the purpose of the challenges. You are the head, or shall I say the glue, that holds things together. You would be the line of defense to prevent everything from being destroyed. The enemy comes to kill, steal, and destroy. Stay on top of your game. Do not allow this to occur. Not in your home. Not in your community, not your block. Not on your watch. You may be with those that genuinely care about you or not. You can still take part. Even in prayer, you can accomplish much. I know some may not be able to be around their children with baby mama drama. Some may even be on lockdown. I pray that this will still encourage you.

CHAPTER 4
LEGACY

"For I have known him, in order that he may command his children and his household after him, that they keep the way of the Lord, to do righteousness and justice, that the Lord may bring to Abraham what He has spoken to him." Genesis 18:19

A legacy would make many think of someone big, wealthy, and powerful. Often money is left to go to another generation. When someone has this mindset, they are limiting their vision to what is possible to become. A legacy would involve more than just money being passed from one generation to another. It is more than just the skillset of a way of life. All these things are important; however, there is more to a legacy than just these things. When your name is continued along with these things, what you are remembered for will be carried along with it, good or bad.

I think about what God said about Abraham just after God promised him a son. I look at this statement God made about legacy.

> "For I have known him, in order that he may command his children and his household after him, that they keep the way of the Lord, to do righteousness and justice, that the Lord may bring to Abraham what He has spoken to him." Genesis 18:19

God told Abraham the different things that were going to take place in his life and how God was going to bless him and his family. This shows that God had trust in Abraham to keep His way and bring up another generation after him to do the same. As you can see, those other things were just a part of what was going to be left. The legacy that is often mentioned in the Bible is the God of Abraham, Isaac, and Jacob. That is the legacy that Abraham played a major part in. God had a plan for something bigger than Abraham.

> I will make you a great nation; I will bless you And make your name great; And you shall be a blessing. Genesis 12:2

We have content in the book about you, your plan, and finding your purpose. Finding your gifts, talents, and abilities. Now you can think about what they are all for you to do. What is God's bigger picture for your life and those you influence? Always keep in mind that not everything is just for you. Others will be blessed by you and will learn from you. Good or bad, you will have an influence on someone. Another example would be when Paul was speaking to Timothy. He was speaking to him about the line of faith that he comes from. In the one statement, you can tell that a lot was imparted to him by his family. Paul was highlighting the legacy in which Timothy was born.

> ...when I call to remembrance the genuine faith that is in you, which dwelt first in your grandmother Lois and your mother Eunice, and I am persuaded is in you also.
> 2 Timothy 1:5

WHAT IS MY PART?

1. LIVE LONG

Live a long life to influence others. God's Word says that a man's life is 120 years. It can seem this is hard to believe, but your body has been designed to live for 120 years. One of the things that you will need to do as your part is to do things that will allow you to live the long life that God intended for you to live. You will want to take care of the temple that was given to you. Make decisions that are in line with a person that will live a long life.

> **What? know ye not that your body is the temple of the Holy Ghost which is in you, which ye have of God, and ye are not your own? 1 Corinthians 6:19**

Since your body is the temple of the Holy Ghost, you want to take proper care of what has been given to you. Think about an expensive sports car that you would like. You would take care of the car. You would wash the car. Get the oil changed. Put new tires on it when needed. You are more important than the car. You would want to take steps to care for your body to prolong your life. This plays a big part in why it can be hard for some to believe that your body was designed for you to live 120 years. There are people that have lived that long; however, you do hear about them in the media. You need to see yourself living a long life.

> And the Lord said, "My Spirit shall not strive with man forever, for he is indeed flesh; yet his days shall be one hundred and twenty years." Genesis 6:3

> "With long life I will satisfy him, And show him My salvation." Psalm 91:16

Another thing you would need to do is take action on what God has promised you. Some of these things can be harder to accomplish than others. Take the steps as much as you can. You can believe the promises and trust that God will come through on His Word. You can continue to trust God; however, you must act. You may not know how to do it, but you must at least take a step in the right direction. You will need to put some action behind your belief.

> "Honor your father and mother," which is the first commandment with promise..." Ephesians 6:2

Honoring your parents would be a promise that causes you to take action. Many promises in God's Word come with conditions. We will have to do our part to ensure the conditions are met. Those were a few scriptures regarding us living a long life as part of leaving a legacy. Another thing we can do to live long is to watch what we eat. God's Word spells out what is clean and what is unclean. The Bible can guide us on what is good to eat and what we are to avoid. Exercise is another way to prolong our lives. Include exercise and eating the right things and make this a regular habit. By doing this, you will have to create a good lifestyle. That will be part of the positive influence you would want to have on others to help them to prolong their lives. You do not have to look at this as if it is a chore. Find something that you like to do, and it will be easier to make it part of your lifestyle. It might be playing a sport, weight lifting, or running. Whatever the case may be, find something that you like to do.

We talked about things that could be done to live long. The next item is for you to teach the next generation. All the things mentioned and outlined in this book can be shared with the next generation to help them to be prepared. Many that are reading this may not have grown up with the right example set before their eyes. Many may not have been in a home where a father was in place to lead the way. If you have never had an example, you can be the example. You can lead the way.

2. TEACH THE NEXT GENERATION.

> "Train up a child in the way he should go, And when he is old he will not depart from it." Proverbs 22:6

The things you do will be passed down to others, whether or not they are good or bad. As you are setting the right example before children while they are young, you are a part of building a strong foundation. Do not take it lightly. There can be many that you come across that are not exposed to the things of God or even know how they operate. For some, you might be the only man of God they may see. All too often, the wrong example is put before their eyes. It can be the community, social media, peers, and other negative examples they're bombarded with day and night. I say the next generation because it would be more than just your children. As the old proverb says, "It takes a village to raise a child."

When thinking about a pack or a group moving forward, I find it interesting when thinking about the contrast between wild animals and humans. The animal I am thinking about is the wolf in the wild. The wolf is a territorial animal. The wolves would be together in a pack. To survive, the wolves would have to hunt prey. They would have to work together to get the big prey. Some wolves can chase their prey up to 40 miles. One wolf can communicate with the others with a howl that can be as far out as ten miles. We always thought the wolves were howling at the moon. This is their form of communication with the others in the pack. Many of the wolves are on the endangered species list due to their lives being taken by man. When this is done to the males, it makes it harder for the others to get the big prey. Especially a mother that has young ones. This causes an impact due to the lack of a team working together to get desired prey to eat. They would be forced to eat the smaller prey because this would be what they could manage better in hunting.

We can look at this similarly when it comes to mankind. Humans can be territorial. They can work together for everyone to move forward. They can all communicate. The village can work and raise the children as a unit; however, when the man is out of the home for whatever reason, the home is impacted. Things are harder for others. Just as the female would not be able to get the bigger, more desired prey, the mother left with the male out of the picture will have a harder time trying to manage the bigger prey. She would have to manage the smaller prey in order to survive. The lifestyle would change due to the impact. This would affect the children and the things that they would have to face. I know we were talking about teaching the next generation, but there is a lesson that can be learned by the wolves.

3. BE IN THE LIVES OF YOUR CHILDREN

When the man is out of the home, there is an impact. The home is impacted if you commit a crime and go to jail. The family could be impacted if you get mad and hit someone out of emotion. Be sure that you manage your emotions. If you are killed, the family will be impacted. If you are caught up in drugs, the family will be impacted. If you commit adultery, the family will be impacted. The decisions that you make can have an impact on the family. You have to be careful before you make decisions. Those decisions are not the right decisions you want to teach the next generation. The things that you would want to teach them would be the positive things that you would walk out. Not only just going to church but being involved in church. Attending the PTA meetings and having a voice. Taking part in the community. Volunteering to help organizations in the community. When you are seen in this light, it can really make a significant difference. This is the type of example that you would want to set.

This is not to single out the man. Women can do the same things. There would also be an impact when the women participate in harmful activities. It is just as important that the woman is not involved in these activities. The consequences would be the same, or in some cases, even worse.

4. TAKE YOUR DOMINION

As the man, you will be attacked. As mentioned in the other chapters, you're the glue that holds it together. When it comes to those that want to break up the home, they attack the head. As the head, we should not allow this to happen. You must think and not get into your emotions. Know the true source that the attack is coming from.

> **The thief does not come except to steal, and to kill, and to destroy. I have come that they may ha ve life, and that they may have it more abundantly. John 10:10**
> Once you realize what is occurring and where the attack is

coming from, adjust and address everything accordingly. Operate in the authority/dominion that has been given to you. You can ask for wisdom and wait for God's response. Then address that situation according to the instructions He provides. It will be vital for you to develop your relationship with God to be sensitive to get His direction. He speaks to us through His Word. Just a rule for you. Know that God will never speak to you to do something outside of His Word. He will not contradict His Word. These are four things that you can keep in mind.

NATURAL AND SPIRITUAL LEGACY

Families were known for what they did in the community. There were many that were known for their skill set, but it is just as important for spiritual life. Think about it. Jesus was a son of man. He was also a son of a carpenter. David was a king, but he was also a man after God's own heart. There is a group of people that were mentioned in the book of Hebrews chapter 11. It is interesting to see how they are remembered more for what was accomplished by their faith than for their occupation. God has so much more for you.

A person's gift can make room for them. The talent, gifts, or skill set will be a platform where God can get credit for the accomplishments that are made. People will ask how you did it. How did you reach this accomplishment? You can point to God and tell them how God helped you. As it is said, every man can preach in his own world. Accomplishments can show God's goodness in and of itself. When you seek God and His direction and instructions on how to do things, work as unto the Lord. Operate in excellence. Allow God to give you insight into the situations. You will be surprised about the outcomes.

How will you be an influence on those around you? What you

do would be part of God's plan and purpose for your life. Do not forget the spiritual part of what your purpose is to accomplish. The spiritual element would be the part of the equation to help you to succeed. There is a success that man would call success, and there is a success that God would call good success. You will not have to compromise for this good success, and you will not have to cheat or step on people to get this success. This success would be wrapped up in God's will for your life. You do not have to prove anything to anyone else. God's opinion is all that matters.

What will be your legacy? Who will they be helping? What value will they add to mankind?

A natural legacy and a spiritual legacy. Think about it. Paul was a Roman brought up around scholars. His life changed, and he was a tentmaker. He was also a believer. The things that he wrote by the Spirit are still being read by millions of people thousands of years later. Luke was a doctor, and he was a believer.

The sons of Issachar were men who understood the times and knew what Israel should do. As you can see, the sons of Issachar were able to add great value and influence others.

> **And their brethren among all the families of Issachar were valiant men of might, reckoned in all by their genealogies fourscore and seven thousand. 1 Chronicles 7:5**

> **And of the children of Issachar, which were men that had understanding of the times, to know what Israel ought to do; the heads of them were two hundred; and all their brethren were at their commandment. 1 Chronicles 12:32**

Just as God was able to use the sons of Issachar, your legacy can be the same or better. We are just not able to do it without God. So give some serious thought to your future and the future of your family.

WRAP UP

He has made us a kingdom of priests. Aim to live long, care for the temple, eat right, and exercise. Teach the next generation. There is a working legacy and a spiritual legacy. You would want to consistently think about the next generation and other generations that are to come. You will want to prepare for what is ahead. Just as a business owner would duplicate himself or a franchise would duplicate itself across the globe. Duplicate Christ in yourself first, then in those that you would influence. Don't build something that will be easily taken away. As mentioned, build a strong foundation. This would be part of building a strong foundation. Just as important as it is to have a skill.

> "A good man leaves an inheritance to his children's children, But the wealth of the sinner is stored up for the righteous." Proverbs 13:22

> "A good name is to be chosen rather than great riches, Loving favor rather than silver and gold." Proverbs 22:1

> "Be diligent to know the state of your flocks, and attend to your herds…" Proverbs 27:23

The decisions that are made today will greatly impact your tomorrow. Everything from the food you eat, the job you take, the friends you select, and even the influences you allow in your life. All of this would have an impact on you and the generations that are coming behind you. Some families can trace their family history to the first relative entering the country. I know not everyone can do so. A new legacy can start with you. There may have been a curse that has been on the family for generations. You are set free from the curse because you are a new creature in Christ. A new legacy can start with you, regardless of how things look right now.

CHAPTER 5
LEADER

> "Indeed I have given him as a witness to the people, A leader and commander for the people." Isaiah 55:3-4

It is important to know that you are a leader and not a follower. However, you will have to be a follower before you can become an effective leader. It is easy to jump into any and everything. Just because it looks one way and sounds one way does not mean that you are dealing with the truth. Just because it sounds good and looks good does not mean that you have the right information. As a leader, you will need to do the research and footwork before coming to a conclusion. Most importantly, do not make decisions based on emotion. Get the insight. When working with knowledge and the truth, you can confidently move forward. You will be able to make better decisions.

> "Be diligent to present yourself approved to God, a worker who does not need to be ashamed, rightly dividing the word of truth." Timothy 2:15

> "So then, my beloved brethren, let every man be swift to hear, slow to speak, slow to wrath." James 1:19

When I think about a leader in my experience, I think about one of my managers from when I worked as a teenager. I was working in a restaurant at the airport in the city where I grew up in Charlotte, North Carolina. His name was Jim. He would wear a shirt and tie every day and face the lines of customers coming through to get their meals. I would be in the back washing the dishes. If I got behind, Jim would come back and help me. This man would tuck his tie in his shirt, roll up his sleeves, stick his hand down deep in the greasy dishwater, and pull out the dishes to be placed on a rack to run through the dishwasher. I wanted to take on this part because of how he was dressed; however, he insisted on taking it on. Not only would he do any and everything that he asked you to do, but he would also demonstrate it time and time again. Not only was he not afraid of getting his hands dirty, but he would take the lead in getting his hands dirty. Jim's actions always stuck with me. He always walked around with a handkerchief in his pocket because he would always use it to wipe his sweat from everything he did all day. The man WORKED HARD!

When thinking about a leader from the Bible, I think about who God called a leader. This person made many mistakes in his lifetime, but God called him a leader and a commander of the people. We can say even after he made so many mistakes, he was still a man after God's own heart. Meaning he wanted what God wanted. He developed a relationship with God to conduct what God wanted him to do. David had some pull. David had some profound influence. That can be seen in the verse in the book of Isaiah with what God mentioned.

> Incline your ear, and come to Me.
> Hear, and your soul shall live;
> And I will make an everlasting covenant with you—
> The sure mercies of David.
> Indeed I have given him as a witness to the people,
> A leader and commander for the people. Isaiah 55:3-4

Imagine that you have this on your resume. Whatever the company is, they can find a place to put you to work. Even if you are to go into business for yourself, you can accomplish a lot knowing that you have this ability. As you develop with the things in the spiritual world, you will be able to do the same in your area of talents and abilities. You will be able to incline your ear and hear the instructions that are provided to you and see amazing results. Have a track record of doing this, and you will have the pull and influence like David.

Here is an example of how David was able to incline his ear and hear to be instructed by God. The families of David and his men were all taken captive by their enemy. The men that David was leading wanted to kill him out of the frustration of their families being taken captive.

> **Now David was greatly distressed, for the people spoke of stoning him, because the soul of all the people was grieved, every man for his sons and his daughters. But David strengthened himself in the Lord his God. Then David said to Abiathar the priest, Ahimelech's son, "Please bring the ephod here to me." And Abiathar brought the ephod to David. So David inquired of the Lord, saying, "Shall I pursue this troop? Shall I overtake them?" And He answered him, "Pursue, for you shall surely overtake them and without fail**

> recover all." So David went, he and the six hundred men who were with him, and came to the Brook Besor, where those stayed who were left behind. But David pursued, he and four hundred men; for two hundred stayed behind, who were so weary that they could not cross the Brook Besor. 1 Samuel 30:6-9

The influence was so strong that the men went from an angry discussion of stoning David to death to following him to recover all. To be able to do this, they must have known that David could hear from God. There had to be a track record of him being able to do this time and time again. They put their lives on the line to follow someone they were just talking about stoning to death.

We have people in our lives who do the same things for us that David did for the men he was leading—everyday people who work to provide direction for us, protect us and preserve our lives and even the lives of our families. Yet, they can be overlooked time and time again. Pastors, priests, parents, mentors, prophets, teachers, and prayer partners, just to name a few. If only we had a record to see all of the things that were avoided because of all the things they have done. All the prayers that they prayed. I am sure their labor was not in vain.

DOMINION

As a man, it would be important that you take your dominion in every situation and circumstance. This may seem like a phrase often said, but not everyone knows what it means. Think about a building with a person working security for the building. There would be an outline or guide on what they can do. Anything from a whistle to a gun. Everything will be outlined as to the process or procedure for the security to follow. What laws are not to be broken to keep them out of trouble? They stick to a process and follow the process.

In the same regard, you will have a similar approach to addressing things that would occur in your life, family, job, church, and other places or groups you take part in. For example, if someone is in the building illegally, the security person would have them leave by following the process outlined in the guide. We have the Word of God. The Bible. This is our guide, or shall we say, a manual for our life as to what the process is that we are to take. It tells us our rights and promises that we are entitled to that God has already provided. In the following passage, Jesus gave believers authority.

> **"Behold, I give you the authority to trample on serpents and scorpions, and over all the power of the enemy, and nothing shall by any means hurt you." Luke 10:19**

Take dominion as part of the things that we evaluate that are taking place around us or even in us. We take the authority that has been provided by God and address it. If there is a lack of money, we take our dominion and speak to it. Claim the promises that God has provided. Just make sure that the conditions are met before we can claim the promises to take place. The leader will need to take dominion over the different things that come against God's purpose. I would encourage you to put this into practice now at whatever state you are in currently. Single. Married. Complicated. A youth. Whatever the situation. I would encourage you to put this into practice now. You will want to develop in this area and in the knowledge of God's Word. You will grow by reading the Bible, praying, and attending church. I know this has been heard repeatedly, but this helps to learn God's character. The more we know about His character, the more we understand how to operate with God.

It was mentioned about making a regular evaluation of the different things in life, such as the company we keep, family, health, and other things of the sort. Those things are to be addressed. They are very important, but often we only address them in the natural. Taking dominion would be addressing them in the spiritual realm. It's important to address in the spirit first, regardless of how crazy it may sound or look. We take dominion in the spiritual world and put a stop to it there, then address it in the natural and put a stop to it in the natural world. Take full dominion.

"You will also declare a thing, And it will be established for you; So light will shine on your ways." Job 22:28

When thinking about how a person sells drugs or controls all the activity in their territory, they will take all the authority given to them and then some. They will be sure to hold things down. They will not allow anyone to come on the block they claim to be theirs. They will show themselves strong and dare anyone to even try them. What is interesting about it is that they will not have a deed of ownership to the property. The street would not be named after them in any way. They may not even live in the neighborhood, but they will lay down their own lives to defend the territory they claim to be theirs. They will lay down their lives for the people that are a part of their group. If someone can take that dominion in that area, the same dominion can be taken when it comes to the home.

Take the same aggression over your home that someone would take over the block they claim and then some. If your child is sick, take the dominion that God has given to you over that sickness. Jump in that just as quickly. Don't allow it to take root. Do not allow it to remain. Just as all that authority has been given to the security guard, the authority has been given to you as a believer to lay hands on the sick and heal them.

> These twelve Jesus sent out and commanded them, saying: "Do not go into the way of the Gentiles, and do not enter a city of the Samaritans. But go rather to the lost sheep of the house of Israel.7. And as you go, preach, saying, 'The kingdom of heaven is at hand.'8. Heal the sick, cleanse the lepers, raise the dead, cast out demons. Freely you have received, freely give." Matthew 10:5-8

> Then He called His twelve disciples together and gave them power and authority over all demons, and to cure diseases. He sent them to preach the kingdom of God and to heal the sick. Luke 9:1-2

> Whatever city you enter, and they receive you, eat such things as are set before you. And heal the sick there, and say to them, 'The kingdom of God has come near to you.' Luke 10:8-9

Just as the twelve were sent, we have the same authority to do the same for our homes, the people around us, or even those we encounter. I know it does not sound like a normal lifestyle. But it can be done. Action has to be taken for it to take effect. It may not be immediate. We will need to act for it to start.

There may be an issue with money. A situation could take place with something that is completely outside of your control. There is nothing too hard for God. At times some are so desperate that they are not even concerned about what people think about them or how they look. They will do what is necessary to accomplish what is needed. All that is needed is to follow the instructions from our guide (The Bible). The instructions are outlined to follow. Give, and it will be given to you. Speak to the situation just as someone speaks to a mountain and causes it to go into the sea. When the instructions are followed, you will be more effective.

> "Give, and it will be given to you: good measure, pressed down, shaken together, and running over will be put into your bosom. For with the same measure that you use, it will be measured back to you." Luke 6:38

> For assuredly, I say to you, whoever says to this mountain, 'Be removed and be cast into the sea,' and does not doubt in his heart, but believes that those things he says will be done, he will have whatever he says. Therefore I say to you, whatever things you ask when you pray, believe that you receive them, and you will have them. Mark 11:23-24

IMPORTANCE OF TAKING DOMINION

There was a time when Adam did not take dominion at a place he should have, and it cost him greatly. Not only did it cost him, but it also impacted many. This is the importance of taking dominion. It impacts more than just you.

INSTRUCTIONS GOD PROVIDED (GUIDE)

> Then the Lord God took the man and put him in the garden of Eden to tend and keep it. And the Lord God commanded the man, saying, "Of every tree of

the garden you may freely eat; but of the tree of the knowledge of good and evil you shall not eat, for in the day that you eat of it you shall surely die." Genesis 2:15-17

WHAT TOOK PLACE (DISOBEDIENCE)

Then the serpent said to the woman, "You will not surely die. For God knows that in the day you eat of it your eyes will be opened, and you will be like God, knowing good and evil." So when the woman saw that the tree was good for food, that it was pleasant to the eyes, and a tree desirable to make one wise, she took of its fruit and ate. She also gave to her husband with her, and he ate. Then the eyes of both of them were opened, and they knew that they were naked; and they sewed fig leaves together and made themselves coverings. Genesis 3:4-7

This was a place where Adam could have referenced the instructions given to him by God. His dominion could have been used, and the issue addressed. Adam could have just followed the instructions provided, and that would have kept everyone safe. Instead, this was a turn that was outside of God's will. It can be challenging when you want to stand for what is right. Pressure can come from every direction. At times it can seem that you are all alone. But God will back you up when you stand on the guide and follow His process. You don't have to settle for anything less than God's best.

There was another example that took place where someone did follow the instructions that God provided. A lot of opposition came against them, but they continued to move forward with what God told them to do. He did not change his mission because of what was happening around him. He stayed consistent with the instructions that were provided to him. This is where Adam fell short.

INSTRUCTIONS GOD PROVIDED (GUIDE).

(God tells Moses to bring His people out of Egypt.)

> And the Lord said: "I have surely seen the oppression of My people who are in Egypt, and have heard their cry because of their taskmasters, for I know their sorrows. So I have come down to deliver them out of the hand of the Egyptians, and to bring them up from that land to a good and large land, to a land flowing with milk and honey, to the place of the Canaanites and the Hittites and the Amorites and the Perizzites and the Hivites and the Jebusites. Now therefore, behold, the cry of the children of Israel has come to Me, and I have also seen the oppression with which the Egyptians oppress them. Come now, therefore, and I will send you to Pharaoh that you may bring My people, the children of Israel, out of Egypt." Exodus 3:7-10

WHAT TOOK PLACE (OBEDIENCE)

> Thus all the children of Israel did; as the Lord commanded Moses and Aaron, so they did. And it came to pass, on that very same day, that the Lord brought the children of Israel out of the land of Egypt according to their armies. Exodus 12:50-51

Moses was sent to Pharaoh to bring the children of Israel out of

Egypt. There was much opposition when Moses walked out what was told to him, but he brought the children out. Even after the children were brought out, they had more opposition. There was a promise of a land flowing with milk and honey. They still had to fight for the land. As a leader, you will find opposition to the promises given, and you will have to fight for them to come to pass. Start with the fight in the spirit, get the instructions from the Spirit, and then walk them out in the natural. I know this sounds like it is far out there, but as you develop your relationship with God, you will begin to understand it better. The enemies of your dream and assignments will not roll out the red carpet to let you walk all over them. In the process, you will need to remember what God has promised. Plan for the opposition. Just because you have God on your side does not mean that everything will be on EASY street. You have a part to play. Even though Moses said he could not do it, with God, he could accomplish what he thought was impossible.

There is still a command that was given to all, and that can be followed today. If you truly want to be a BOSS. We can all follow the command that God gave in His Word long before Moses. This is part of the authority that has been given to us. Just as we can dominate with a basketball on the court, with a football on the field, or we can win the boxing title in the ring, so can we dominate by taking dominion over our homes, families, communities, church, jobs, and wherever we go. Be the BOSS that God intended for you to be in everyday life.

> **Then God blessed them, and God said to them, "Be fruitful and multiply; fill the earth and subdue it; have dominion over the fish of the sea, over the birds of the air, and over every living thing that moves on the earth." Genesis 1:28**

WRAP UP

Just as many would hold things down to take care of their block or territory, the man can hold things down for his home. Address the things in the spiritual world, which in turn will have the power to change the things in the natural world. If you don't like what you are experiencing, change it in the spirit first. Just as an eagle considers how to build a strong foundation, man can do the same. Our communities are counting on us. God is counting on us. You have more intelligence than a bird. God can take care of you in many different ways than a bird. You are the head and not the tail. I encourage you to move forward in that direction if you have not already.

> **"And the Lord will make you the head and not the tail; you shall be above only, and not be beneath, if you heed the commandments of the Lord your God which I command you today, and are careful to observe them."**
> **Deuteronomy 28:13**

CHAPTER 6
MANAGING PRESSURE

"We are hard-pressed on every side, yet not crushed; we are perplexed, but not in despair..." 2 Corinthians 4:8

Some things challenge people in different ways. When pressure is applied to what is on the inside, it comes out. The Bible clearly states that out of the abundance of the heart, the mouth speaks. Don't allow the pressures to cause you to react in the wrong way. I remember when my uncle would tell me about my grandfather in the home when they were growing up. He talked about how he may have been hard at times. When my uncle got older, he understood better what my grandfather was going through. He was working a job all day long where people could do wrong things to him and treat him wrong. He had to stay quiet to keep the job. He had to hold his peace and not jeopardize his job. He had a family to feed. So what that meant is that when someone would face challenges like this, they would come home and take it out on their family or the loved ones they lived with.

We all have to be careful with our words and our actions. We can apologize for our actions and attempt to take back our words, but it does not take away the hurt they cause. Just a mental note here. There is a lot of good that can be done after the fact. People always remember the bad things that were done.

> **My brethren, count it all joy when you fall into various trials, knowing that the testing of your faith produces patience. But let patience have its perfect work, that you may be perfect and complete, lacking nothing. James 1:2-4**

Daniel had a point in his life where there was a great amount of pressure placed on him. His very life was in jeopardy. A group of individuals did not like Daniel. They put a plan together to come against Daniel. There was a decree made that if any man asked anything of any other god and not the king, they would be put in the lion's den. They knew that the one thing that would stay consistent about Daniel would be regarding him and his God. Daniel had a relationship with God that was so tight he did not let a decree come between him and his relationship with God.

(WICKED PLAN)

> **All the governors of the kingdom, the administrators and satraps, the counselors and advisors, have consulted together to establish a royal statute and to make a firm decree, that whoever petitions any god or man for thirty days, except you, O king, shall be cast into the den of lions. Now, O king, establish the decree and sign the writing, so that it cannot be changed, according to the law of the Medes and Persians, which**

does not alter." Therefore King Darius signed the written decree. Daniel 6:7-9

(DANIEL STAYED THE SAME)

Now when Daniel knew that the writing was signed, he went home. And in his upper room, with his windows open toward Jerusalem, he knelt down on his knees three times that day, and prayed and gave thanks before his God, as was his custom since early days. Then these men assembled and found Daniel praying and making supplication before his God. And they went before the king, and spoke concerning the king's decree: "Have you not signed a decree that every man who petitions any god or man within thirty days, except you, O king, shall be cast into the den of lions?" The king answered and said, "The thing is true, according to the law of the Medes and Persians, which does not alter." Daniel 6:10-12

Daniel did not allow the pressure that was being placed on him to stop him in any way. He stayed consistent with his relationship with God, even openly in front of everyone. I see people making silent prayers or praying behind closed doors where no one can see, but Daniel did it openly. I find it very inspiring to see someone put their faith in God over the situation or the circumstances that they are facing. Daniel was placed in the lion's den against the king's wishes. The king knew that the decree could not be altered. He was concerned about Daniel.

(SAVED FROM THE LION'S DEN WITHOUT HARM)

> Now the king went to his palace and spent the night fasting; and no musicians were brought before him. Also his sleep went from him. Then the king arose very early in the morning and went in haste to the den of lions. And when he came to the den, he cried out with a lamenting voice to Daniel. The king spoke, saying to Daniel, "Daniel, servant of the living God, has your God, whom you serve continually, been able to deliver you from the lions?" Then Daniel said to the king, "O king, live forever! My God sent His angel and shut the lions' mouths, so that they have not hurt me, because I was found innocent before Him; and also, O king, I have done no wrong before you." **Daniel 6:18-22**

God protected Daniel in the lion's den the entire night. I wonder if the king was worried more than Daniel. God performed a miracle for Daniel. He got his victory, and it can be noticed that he did not compromise. He did not change who he was to fit in with the crowd. He was willing to stand alone if he needed to do it alone. He put his priorities in place and stuck to what he believed.

(ENEMIES OUTCOME)

> "And the king gave the command, and they brought those men who had accused Daniel, and they cast them into the den of lions—them, their children, and their wives; and the lions overpowered them, and broke all their bones in pieces before they ever came to the bottom of the den." **Daniel 6:24**

When people come up against the people of God, they are not aware of what they are doing. It's not a clever idea. The outcome will not go well.

Jesus was also under a tremendous amount of pressure when facing what He was about to go through on the cross.

> **Coming out, He went to the Mount of Olives, as He was accustomed, and His disciples also followed Him. When He came to the place, He said to them, "Pray that you may not enter into temptation." And He was withdrawn from them about a stone's throw, and He knelt down and prayed, saying, "Father, if it is Your will, take this cup away from Me; nevertheless not My will, but Yours, be done." Then an angel appeared to Him from heaven, strengthening Him. And being in agony, He prayed more earnestly. Then His sweat became like great drops of blood falling down to the ground. Luke 22:39-44**

He was going to suffer on the cross and was taking time in prayer to prepare Himself for what was to come. This is a good example that we can learn from before facing a difficult situation. Jesus knew He was going to die and that He was going to suffer before His death. Nevertheless, He said, "Not My will, but Yours be done." Even though He knew it was going to be difficult, He was still obedient to God's will for His life. Even in the challenging part of His life, the people closest to Him were not backing Him up as He would have liked. He was praying intensely, and they were falling asleep. Another one was right in the process of betraying Him. Jesus knew that He was going to be betrayed. Yet, He still pursued the Father's will.

We may not be faced with a life-threatening situation, but it is still important that we do not allow different pressures to force us into the wrong situations. For example, the pressure can come for you to have the things others have in their possession.

FORGIVENESS

Although things can negatively affect you, you can choose to forgive. I know this is easier said than done. When you look at what occurs in the news, this is not often practiced. I get it. People are not trying to hear about forgiveness unless they are asking for it. One out of every two adults has experienced incarceration in their family. When looking at TV, listening to certain music, or watching many movies, they tell you to strike back over everything. It can even be seen on the playground at a young age. A fight is instigated to have entertainment for everyone's amusement. As they grow older, they want attention and often brag about how they do not care. Here is the problem. They need to start caring. Caring about their life. Care about the other person's life and the life of others. According to the FBI Uniform Crime Reporting Program in 2020, out of all the different types of crimes that went up, murder went up the most. That is nationwide. People can always make comments from the sideline like, "I know you are not going to take that off of them." "I would not take that." Do not be worried about what people will think about you. Stay consistent and do the right thing. There is a time and place to defend yourself and those in your care. Make sure you are in the right mindset before taking action.

> "And whenever you stand praying, if you have anything against anyone, forgive him, that your Father in heaven may also forgive you your trespasses." Mark 11:25

Here is the thing. It does not cost them anything to get people at odds with one another. A show is put on for them, and they have something to talk about for the next few weeks. It costs them nothing. What does it cost you? Money for court costs. Time away from your family. Criminal record. Limited job opportunities. Who is really paying the price here? The adrenaline may be flowing, but you are better off knowing that the cost is a lot more than what you are seeing at the current time. As it is said, sin will cost you more than you intended to pay and cause you to stay longer than you intended to stay. You do not have to make a name for yourself by putting on a show for people. God's Word says that He will make your name great. Start respecting people. Start respecting their property. Stay out of their business and mind your own. Teach others to do the same. That will keep a lot of people out of trouble.

> "A man of great wrath will suffer punishment; For if you rescue him, you will have to do it again." Proverbs 19:19

> "There are many plans in a man's heart, Nevertheless the Lord's counsel—that will stand." Proverbs 19:21

One evening I was walking out of the library and ran into one of the people from the old neighborhood. He was known to be one of the people that you would not mess with in any way. He was cool. You know he was one of the people who did not get his reputation by being Mr. Nice Guy. He asked what I was doing. I told him I had a temporary job at a bank. He looked me in the eye and paused. Then he said, "You better stick with that." It was his way of encouraging me. His wife and children came out, and he introduced me to them, and then he made the same statement.

"You better stick with that." There are times you must hear what someone is telling you. Not only what they are telling you but also what they are showing you. He had just got off work, and it looked like a very labor-intensive job. He was tired but was telling me in a way that all the things that he did when he was younger cost him in the long run. He was limited as to what he could do to bring home an income due to the fact that he had a record. Not to say that he was bad off, but you could tell it was a challenging time for him and his family. They were making work. Those things that were done in the past were not worth what he was going through at that time. You don't have to be the biggest and the baddest. You don't have to put your future and the future of others at risk.

The pressure can be there for you to get people back. People can look at you like you are weak. Is your reputation worth more than your future? If you are being recorded on the phone for someone to post on social media, they are not your friend. We often see someone in a challenging situation, and the person taking the video is not helping them in any way. People on the sidelines can say anything that they want. Remember that it does not cost them anything. It takes more courage to resolve conflict in a positive way. Society would want you to take out one another. It takes more heart to preserve a life.

COMPARING YOURSELF WITH OTHERS

Do not allow the challenges to take you off of your faith. Many can carry out an assignment while having to deal with the different things they face in their personal lives. There are many examples of this in the Bible. There are some that people can see clearly from how it was spelled out in the Bible. There are some things that there is no record about. You do not have to look far with all that is taking place at this point and time. Comparing yourself to others can make you feel like you are missing something. Then pressure can come from others to go into debt to have what everyone else seems to have, but do they really have these things? Do they have the things, or do the things have them? We do not know how they got the things they have in their possession. Will they have to take time away from their families to pay for these things that they just have to have? Will it take time away from you developing yourself in other areas to bring in more income? Most importantly, does it take away from your time with God by attending church, understanding His Word, and growing spiritually? Pressure can come from your lust, your wife, your friends, or even your children. How much does it really cost you long term? Will the things have you, or will you have them and be able to keep everything else intact? You don't have to go that route to have success. You do not have to get in debt or take from anyone. You can seek God for it and get it His way. It would be in a way that would be on a stronger foundation.

There was a restaurant owner that was standing in line at the bank one day. He was very discouraged. Wondering how to make ends meet. Not knowing how things would turn out for his business. I know this can be discouraging when the other restaurants are established and running well, and you see your potential customers go to the competitors. There was another restaurant owner that came to the bank and got in the same line. The second restaurant owner began to encourage the first restaurant owner while they both waited in line at the bank. The second restaurant owner was telling his story about how he worked in his restaurant for ten years without a profit. They keep going to keep the restaurant afloat. They stayed consistent and now have several locations in the same city and continue to grow today. He stayed consistent, and he stayed focused. If it is something that you know God has set out for you to do, let that motivate you to keep going. Make sure you have the right motives for what you are doing. Be sure it is for the right reason. Let God be the One to bless, and be sure you are not getting so ambitious that you start compromising in areas like your integrity, family, friends, etc. Trust God. He will open the door.

> "Do not overwork to be rich; Because of your own understanding, cease!" Proverbs 23:4

> "I will make you a great nation; I will bless you And make your name great; And you shall be a blessing." Genesis 12:2

A person's gift can make room for them. The talent, gifts, or skill set will be a platform where God can get credit for your accomplishments. People will ask how you did it. You can point to God and tell them how God helped you. As it is said, let every man preach in his own world. When you seek God and His direction and instructions on how to do things, work as unto the Lord. Operate in excellence. Allow God to give you insight into the situations that you face. There can be obstacles that may come to you or the group that you are a part of. They can see how God is with you as you manage things properly. The groups that you work with would begin to want to know more about the God that you serve. You will be surprised about the outcomes.

PEER PRESSURE

Pressure can be from those that you are around at work, family, friends, or others. They might try to make you feel weak or that you are not a man if you do not have a flock of women or do the wrong things that they do. Take a close look at the person that is saying that and look at their present condition. Think about what they are headed to in the future. Keep all that in mind when they are trying to get you to consider their advice.

Think of a child in a candy store. They have a tough time making a choice. It can be a challenge to make a decision with so many types of candy and flavors to choose from. This can be a hard process for the Bad Boy. If he commits at any point, he will feel that he is missing out on everything else. He will want to have a long list of experiences before he settles. If he ever chooses to settle. Yes, the Bad Boy would be a player. This will be a bad thing because the feelings and emotions of all will be damaged. This will cause baggage to be brought to future relationships. If there are children involved, that could amplify the damage that is caused.

King Solomon had 700 wives and 300 concubines (1 Kings 11:3). I am sure he had fun as a King with this many women at his beck and call. Sadly, they led him away from his destiny. When the time came for responsibility, one can only imagine how hard it would have been for him to spend time with the wives and children. There are only 365 days in a year. Not to say that Solomon was a bad man. He could easily be seen as an absentee father to his children if he had so many by these different women. Some say he may have married some of the women to make allies with other kingdoms to prevent wars, even though there was not a war with his kingdom during his time as king. This could have been managed better.

It is interesting to note that in the book of Proverbs and the book of Ecclesiastes, there are verses about that one special woman.

> "May your fountain be blessed and may you rejoice in the wife of your youth." Proverbs 5:18

> "Live joyfully with the wife whom you love all the days of your vain life which He has given you under the sun, all your days of vanity; for that is your portion in life, and in the labor which you perform under the sun."
> Ecclesiastes 9:9

It sounds like there is a lesson to learn about a man that is with one woman for a long time. It appears Solomon still learned a lesson despite having all the women the Bad Boy could dream of having.

This can be one relationship without all the baggage from all the others piling in and impacting the true God-given, God-ordained future where it would be easier for the destiny that the two will become one. More focus could be put on the marriage with fewer distractions outside the marriage such as other women, past girlfriends, baby mamas, past hurts, and drama coming from every direction. Even the wise man in the Bible learned something. Please learn from him and not bow down to the pressure of making the wrong decision. Do it God's way. Get the wife that He chooses for you. It impacts more than you.

COMMUNICATION WITH GOD

There is a message being sent (Prayer). A message to be received (Are you listening?). Yes. God is trying to tell you something. You must take the time to remove all distractions and develop a sensitivity to hearing God. Do not only remove distractions but quiet your mind. Do not let thoughts continue to run in your mind, and sit there and respond to them in your head. Quiet your mind. It is like you are trying to tune a radio to that frequency to get that radio station. You do not just pray and walk away. Are you listening? Develop that relationship to tap into that right frequency. Just like the radio station may not play the song that you want to hear when you want to hear it, God may not tell you what you want to hear when you want to hear it. Realize that God has your best interests at heart. Be honest with yourself. It is essential that you develop yourself spiritually in this area.

> "He who has ears to hear, let him hear!" Matthew 11:15

We want to be able to hear. We need to hear what God is saying. We need to know what the Spirit of God is trying to tell us. Seeking God first can help us receive His guidance on what and how things need to be presented. When to speak and when you need to be quiet. It will be God's will for you to be effective at communicating, not only with God but also with others.

> "Let your speech always be with grace, seasoned with salt, that you may know how you ought to answer each one." Colossians 4:6

WRAP UP

Although you can face some things that others do not know about, and challenges can be many, you need to remember that you are not alone. You can go on and on and do things with the intelligence that you have to accomplish what you can accomplish. When you operate out of an emotional response to the pressure on you, you limit your intelligence because you are in an emotion. The actions that are taken will not be able to be reversed. The words said cannot be erased. Be slow to speak and swift to hear. Don't be quick to fly off the handle to take action. Evaluate the entire situation first. Make sure that you know the whole truth, regardless if you hear the audio or see a video. You may only be looking at one part. Make sure you have the whole truth. No matter where the pressure comes from to push you in a certain direction, don't allow the pressure to break you. Keep your focus on God and His direction. Do not be moved.

CHAPTER 7
DEVELOP YOURSELF

A man's gift makes room for him, And brings him before great men. Proverbs 18:16

HAVE A PLAN

In society today, many can be seen as they go and do the same thing from day to day. They can only be concerned with what is in front of them now. That is a limited line of sight. It is like someone taking life as it comes and not preparing for what is ahead. Not to say everything in the future will be bad, but it is good to prepare. If you have dreams for good things to occur, you will want to plan for them. If you sense there will be challenges ahead, seek God on how to prepare yourself and others. What are you set out to do, and what steps will you take to get there?

PURPOSE

Where do you see yourself in the next five years? I know it is asked so often. Job interviews. Dating conversation. Explanation to parents. Elevator speeches to give with major leaders. This is very important to have. Not just a cliché or a nice speech to recite whenever you are asked. You will need an actual vision, a plane with a purpose. The reason why is that you don't just exist. You are here for a purpose.

> **Where there is no vision, the people perish: but he that keepeth the law, happy is he. Proverbs 29:18**

You can't do everything for everyone. When this is done, it can take away from your goals, plans, and the quality of what you are to provide. You must take time to evaluate and ask, "Is this going to take me off track? Will this be a distraction? Will this task cost me time, money, and effort that can be better used to accomplish my purpose? It may not seem like it at the time. This will influence others and not just yourself. You cannot be in a state where you are performing for something other than what your skills, gifts, talents, and abilities have been set for you to do. What are you called to do?

DO NOT BE DISCOURAGED

Find out what you can do the best with the least amount of effort. Know the purpose. This will bring you closer to knowing what your gift is that was given to you. It can be bigger than what you may do for recreation. There can be things out there that you have not been exposed to up until now. There was a time when the Internet did not exist. There was no way for anyone to be exposed to the Internet or even know any details about the Internet. (Internet. What is that?) However, now there are many careers that someone can consider pursuing. Determine what your gift is and then begin to develop it so that you can become even better at this gift. Take the time to think about your talents, gifts, and abilities. What is the easiest thing you can do with the least amount of effort? This can give you a clue as to what your gift is that God has given you. After reviewing that, you can think about what you are called to do.

Networking is good. Getting an education can be important. Seeking God and His direction for your life would be most important. There's no need to waste time, money, and energy on the wrong things that do not bring you value. Be sure to make your decisions with purpose. A university may not be the direction for you. Playing sports may not be the direction that He has for you. Maybe. Maybe not. Don't just jump into things because they all sound good at the time. Think it through and seek God.

The steps of a good man are ordered by the Lord, And He delights in his way. Psalm 37:23

You will want to continue developing because this will bring you before people who need what you have to offer. You will not want to stay at the same skill set without becoming better. This can be understood with sports or hobbies that someone can have. It is interesting how many can explain this to a child to get the desired position on the sports team, but they will not follow the same advice when it comes to career, spiritual things, relationships with people, and other aspects of life. The more that you develop the gifts, the further they can take you.

A man's gift makes room for him, And brings him before great men. Proverbs 18:16

Education is a good thing to have. It can open many doors for you. However, having knowledge is only one part. At times it is the only part that people think is needed. It takes wisdom to apply the knowledge that you receive. Just because someone has a degree does not guarantee success. Don't be discouraged that others may have higher education than you may have at the current time. Continue to be diligent and consistent and move forward. There are things that add value that many do not think about until it is too late. Integrity, loyalty, and consistency, to name a few.

> **Wisdom is the principal thing; Therefore get wisdom. And in all your getting, get understanding. Proverbs 4:7**

A college degree does not determine or guarantee success. A person can still be successful. A college degree may not be for everyone.

You will want to be with like-minded people. Those that can help you by giving you insight from their experience. This can help you to avoid the mistakes they have made in the past. This will also give you an ally in your field or profession. Now you know what they will always say: "I taught him that!" Iron sharpens iron.

> **As iron sharpens iron, So a man sharpens the countenance of his friend. Proverbs 27:7**

I had the opportunity to take classes at night to learn a different skill. I was fortunate that my job would help some with the finances to take the classes. I remember it like it was yesterday. I went to my manager to get my paperwork signed and approved. It was so good to work for someone that was so supportive of what I was trying to do. It was like she was waving the flag for me to go for the goal. I remember her telling me, "Good for you. Good for you. You can do this now while you do not have all the other things to consider that others have to worry about. You don't have children, and you are not married." She was basically saying you can put your focus on what you are doing and what you are there to accomplish. At that point, others were only concerned about how what I was doing was going to affect them instead of how what I was doing was going to help me develop and move forward. It was refreshing to have someone in my corner.

CO-WORKERS ATTEND SCHOOL IN THE EVENINGS

I had two co-workers that were taking classes at the same time. One co-worker was at my full-time job, and the other co-worker was at my part-time job. The co-worker from my full-time job took all the same courses that I took. We understood the long hours, group projects, and class time to improve. Not only did we learn in school, but we got involved with different programs to use what we learned in our courses and began to teach the next generation. We both were able to get better jobs with more responsibilities and with higher salaries. This placed us both in a better position to do and learn more. We did not have to stop at this same point.

The co-worker at the part-time job was a lifeguard. I was attending for design, and the lifeguard was attending to be a chef. Things began to be a challenge for him financially, and he could no longer attend school. He was able to get a job where he was working under a chef. Everything he was going to learn in school, he was able to learn by working under the chef. It was like he was able to pick right up from where the school had left off. Paying and going to school to learn and develop a skill is one thing. It is another thing to learn a skill set for free. And it is a different thing altogether to learn a skill set and get paid for learning what you love to do. I had not seen someone so excited about what they were doing up until this time in my life. He was working and enjoying what he was doing the whole time, but he would look up and see that the day was done and it was time for him to go home. Then he would be saddened as if he was missing something. People talk about a passion for something. This is a true passion for what you are doing.

So, let's say you have found your gift. Then you act by developing your gift. These steps should align with your passion. You should have a passion for what you are doing. This should be something that you look forward to when you get up, not something that you dread doing. The desire for it should be in your heart for what you are doing. As you develop yourself, the money will come. Work on your craft. As it is said, "If you are doing what you love, you will never work another day in your life."

I know a lot of this is easier said than done. You can find a way to get it done. You can have a relationship with God. Seek His face and look to Him to get the plan and the steps to take. It may not come quickly at first. Continue to seek and press in to get the answers for your steps. There are people that are on lockdown that took advantage of what they could and came out with a degree. All things are possible with God.

> **Jesus said to him, "If you can believe, all things are possible to him who believes." Matthew 9:23**

> **"For with God nothing will be impossible." Luke 1:37**

Do not look at a roadblock and drop everything and say it cannot be done. Not everything that is done will be an easy street. Not everyone will be happy with what you are doing. You have the ability to be beyond the challenge that is in front of you. There are others before us all that accomplished so much regardless of the opposition.

SPIRITUAL

> "This Book of the Law shall not depart from your mouth, but you shall meditate in it day and night, that you may observe to do according to all that is written in it. For then you will make your way prosperous, and then you will have good success." Joshua 1:8

Just as a person can take steps to develop in their career, they can also develop in the spirit. You can develop to the point that you are more sensitive to God and His direction for you and the people that are part of your center of influence. The process would be like a relationship with a person in the natural. You spend time with them. You get to know them. You get to know their character. The more time you spend with them, the better you get to know them. You develop a relationship. A similar process would take place in developing your relationship with God. You will become sensitive to Him and His direction for you. It's important to be sensitive to the help and the leadership that God is giving you. There can be warnings of what not to do. Warnings of who not to be with or who not to be around. Oftentimes, people wait until something bad happens, and then they say, "Something told me."

Develop yourself in the spirit to the point that you can make good, sound decisions long before a problem occurs. God can help you navigate around what He knows is going to occur. It may catch you by surprise, but it will not catch God by surprise. As you can see in the book of Psalms in the Bible, David had to seek God and be led by Him. So what are some things you can do to develop spiritually?

1. PRAY

"...pray without ceasing..." 1 Thessalonians 5:17

"Confess your trespasses to one another, and pray for one another, that you may be healed. The effective, fervent prayer of a righteous man avails much." James 5:16

2. READ THE BIBLE (AS MENTIONED BEFORE)

This Book of the Law shall not depart from your mouth, but you shall meditate in it day and night, that you may observe to do according to all that is written in it. For then you will make your way prosperous, and then you will have good success. Joshua 1:8

3. ATTEND A GOOD BIBLE TEACHING CHURCH

"...not forsaking the assembling of ourselves together, as is the manner of some, but exhorting one another, and so much the more as you see the Day approaching." Hebrews 10:25

What are some things to develop? What are some things to keep in mind?

"Teach me to do Your will, For You are my God; Your Spirit is good. Lead me in the land of uprightness." Psalm 143:10

Develop yourself to the point that you will be able to know the difference between you being led by God or by others. Others can try to get you to do what they want you to do for their benefit. Develop yourself spiritually to know God's voice. Know God's leading. It will help you.

> **To him the doorkeeper opens, and the sheep hear his voice; and he calls his own sheep by name and leads them out. And when he brings out his own sheep, he goes before them; and the sheep follow him, for they know his voice. Yet they will by no means follow a stranger, but will flee from him, for they do not know the voice of strangers. John 10:3-5**

Develop yourself so that you will know if you are trying to do something that is a God-given desire or if it is something that you want and are ignoring what God is leading you to do. God is not obligated to finish what you start on your own.

Develop yourself to know if you are being led by God or if this is just a good idea.

> **"For the word of God is living and powerful, and sharper than any two-edged sword, piercing even to the division of soul and spirit, and of joints and marrow, and is a discerner of the thoughts and intents of the heart." Hebrews 4:12**

You don't have to be moved to act by the things outside of you. Do not bow down to that pressure. Be moved by what is on the inside of you. That would be by what God is leading you to do. It may be hard to believe, but He loves you more than you love yourself. He loves you enough to help you make the right decision even if you do not see it at the time. You may be looking at the wrong thing. You may be thinking about the wrong thing. He is thinking about what is down the road that is headed your way.

He loves you enough for you not to hurt yourself. Sometimes we can think we know what we are doing, but God can see the bigger picture.

Pressures can come. People can have question after question. Circumstance after circumstance can occur. People can all come at the same time to bombard you with information. They will come with a loud voice to try to pressure you to make a quick decision. Realize that this is coming to you in a way that is designed to get a certain reaction from you. It can be either from the person or the wrong spirit that the person is yielding to come at you. Still, be led by God in the situation. Not by the person or the circumstance. I think the following passage is the best example that Jesus demonstrated when He encountered challenges.

> **But Jesus went to the Mount of Olives. Now early in the morning He came again into the temple, and all the people came to Him; and He sat down and taught them. Then the scribes and Pharisees brought to Him a woman caught in adultery. And when they had set her in the midst, they said to Him, "Teacher, this woman was caught in adultery, in the very act. Now Moses, in the law, commanded us that such should be stoned. But what do You say?" This they said, testing Him, that they might have something of which to accuse Him. But Jesus stooped down and wrote on the ground with His finger, as though He did not hear. So when they continued asking Him, He raised Himself up and said to them, "He who is without sin among you, let him throw a stone at her first." And again He stooped down and wrote on the ground. Then those who heard it, being convicted by their conscience, went out one by one, beginning with the oldest even to the last. And**

Jesus was left alone, and the woman standing in the midst. When Jesus had raised Himself up and saw no one but the woman, He said to her, "Woman, where are those accusers of yours? Has no one condemned you?" She said, "No one, Lord." And Jesus said to her, "Neither do I condemn you; go and sin no more." John 8:1-11

Jesus paused, gave an answer, then stooped down again and wrote on the ground. He set the pace. He did not allow the group to pressure or push Him into deciding. Jesus did not even sweat. He handled the situation. Recognize the tactic that the enemy is using against you. Respond to what God is leading you to do. Aim to please Him.

WRAP UP

Have a vision. If you do not have a vision, then work on getting a vision for your life. Do not just roll with the punches and end up somewhere and wonder how you got there. Work on having a plan with a purpose. Find your talents and gifts. Develop them to become better at them. Someone can do a very good job in four hours. Imagine doing a very good job with the same quality in 30 minutes. Regardless of how good we are, there are still ways we can improve. And do not only develop your skills, talents, and abilities but also develop yourself spiritually. Continue to grow consistently and learn to become better in every area.

CHAPTER 8
GATE KEEPERS

15 See then that you walk circumspectly, not as fools but as wise, 16 redeeming the time, because the days are evil. Ephesians 5:15-16

When we see major corporations gated all around, we know they are secure. No one can get in without clearance. It would be the same for corporate buildings in major cities. Visitors would have to come to a security desk. Individuals would have limited access to different areas of the building. Things are organized and put in order. There would be a security desk that would verify the information to keep things in order and keep everyone safe. When living in a gated community or secured apartment building, you can feel safer knowing that everyone will be checked by security before entering. As the leaders of the home, we are the gatekeepers as to what is allowed in our lives and the lives of those for whom we are responsible. That would include everything from the TV to social media to the people that walk through the door of our homes. In a similar way, we are the security of the home, but in so many other ways. To most, this is an area that may not be popular at times, but we have to take our stand to secure our homes, communities, and churches.

PROACTIVE

The watchman on the wall is to be active and alert. They can see the enemies miles ahead to set off the alarm to let everyone know. The trumpet of the warning can be blown. By being a proactive gatekeeper, you can alert the city to get prepared. You can put everyone in a position to defend themselves. The watchman can alert the gatekeeper. The gatekeeper can take up the bridge and lock the gate. Or they can leave the gate down to allow the army to come out to defend. There is teamwork taking place here. You can see that the team is working together to defend the city and keep everyone safe. To be proactive, you will need to think ahead and be prepared.

> **My heart wavered, fearfulness frightened me; The night for which I longed He turned into fear for me. Prepare the table, Set a watchman in the tower, Eat and drink. Arise, you princes, Anoint the shield! For thus has the Lord said to me: set a watchman, Let him declare what he sees." Isaiah 21:4-6**

Now, let's think about this in the home environment today. It is important to know that one cannot be caught sleeping on the job. There are lives of those that are close to you to consider. Often, many sleep or become distracted or have too much on their plate to address the things that should be a priority. You have to remove those things that distract or even prevent those things from coming into your home or from having an influence in your lives or the lives of those that are in your care.

There was a time when I wanted to have a basketball goal in the driveway when I was a youth. My dad told me no. I did not understand at the time. He told me this would bring more people around than we needed to be around the house. As a child, you want something and do not think things through along with the consequences. He was there to help me along these lines. Little did I know that I got to see exactly what he was talking about months to a year later. There were basketball courts around that people could use, but that was a house on a corner with one. People would come and play at any time. The people were not even at home. People did not care. They would play basketball anyway. The owners would tie up the net, but that did not matter. The element was there until the basketball goals were brought down. In the midst of all of this, there were basketball courts that were within walking distance and were open to the public. Those courts were not crowded, and the goals were in good condition. There was no need for everyone to go play on this basketball goal. Now that I am older, I can see that the decision my dad made was the best move for the family. It was not just about me. What I really hate to see is a basketball goal set up and the family that it was intended for not being able to play on it as much as everyone else.

Furthermore, watchmen can anticipate what is coming and take action to get everyone prepared. You may not know what to do right away, but by having a relationship with God, you can receive direction on what to do next. For example, two neighbors live side by side. They can both come home day after day and have the same routine and not be aware of their surroundings. As the gatekeeper, both neighbors can monitor the neighborhood and see everything that is taking place—who is coming in and out of the neighborhood and what activities are happening there. It would be important to know because all of this would have an impact on those that are in their care. Now let's say there is a large gap between the houses. This can be a concern because the gap could be a potential cut-through to get to the street or another area. Something could seem very innocent at the beginning. What could happen with the cut-through is that it could bring more traffic of people cutting in between the houses. After that, you can have trash left around the cut-through between the two houses. The wrong elements can start to hang around the cut-through. There can be traffic that will come through that would start casing the two homes. A good watchman, or shall we say gatekeeper, would be able to see ahead and make provisions. Someone can nip this in the bud by having a gate put up to help keep things secure.

MONITORING

In the past, there were larger families with fewer distractions. Many families were on farms or ranches. The children were too busy working or studying to get into the wrong things. There were not so many items to worry about children being exposed to at an important time of their lives. As the gatekeeper, you will need to monitor so much more. Things inside your house and even outside influences. Monitor and filter what can come in and what has to stay out.

I was over at a friend's house one evening and noticed how he had the remote control handy beside the television. Normally people would think about a man having control and being the only one to change the channel to what they wanted to see, and the family will just have to watch what he is watching. That was not the case. I remember him telling me that afternoon that he had to keep the remote handy and close by because of what might come through the television. He was not only monitoring what was coming from the programs that the family would watch but even the commercials. He would be quick on the draw. We watched the game that afternoon. It is not enough to stop something from coming through; we need to give understanding to those in our care. The commercial for alcohol shows a lot of young people that seem to be having fun. What we do not see is the person that got hooked on this when they were young, and they are up in age now and still drinking the same brand. Now notice that the person that is up in age is not getting cast for the role in the commercial. That would only expose what the addiction to alcohol would lead them to in the future. Being in a position to explain the decisions to give understanding would be a good position for you. My friend was a good example. You know that people will always ask, "But why? I don't understand." Regardless of how others may feel, we have to do the right thing.

> **See then that you walk circumspectly, not as fools but as wise, redeeming the time, because the days are evil.**
> **Ephesians 5:15-16**

There is so much more to think about today. The television is only one of many things. Phones, text, social media, friends, movies, and schools, just to name a few. These are not to be taken for granted. We can not just assume that everything is okay or someone else will handle everything. We are the gatekeepers. I would not want anything bad to happen to anyone, only to find out later and say, "I should have said something." You say, "I should have done something," or even worse, "I did not know this was going on." Everybody knew but you.

Be active and know what social media they are using. Put the things that everyone is doing in an open space. Monitor what is going on. Know who calls are going to and what is being texted. Know where money is being spent. To help you get to know this information, you can have regular inspections. It might not be popular, but you love them enough to check. You want to be sure they do not get themselves into something that they cannot handle. You do not want anything to occur that will impact the family. Even video games online. You need to know what is going on as the gatekeeper. Not to say that you will catch everything, but you can be on your watch.

VALIDATION

I had a friend while in my teenage years. It was someone in the neighborhood that would hang out with us from time to time. We had to go to his house for something, and I met his mother for the first time. I can laugh at it now, but back then, I felt like I was being interrogated. All the questions just keep coming. You can think of the old-school way that they did things. Questions start off with "Who are you?" "Who are your people?" Questions went on and on. His mother could see how I felt. Then she said, I am just trying to know who my son is around. Now I really understand that and see how important that is today. She can validate who I am and see what I am truly about. Over the years, I was amazed at how parents would have different and creative ways to monitor and validate what their children were doing. When I started high school, I remember when my mother and I stepped on campus for the first time. The school I attended was across town. I thought it was too far for her to know what was going on with me being across town. While my mother was there, she saw some people that she knew and made some new friends while she was at the open house. I was not quick enough to catch on to what was being done. My mother was setting things up to have another set of eyes watch over me. I could not have gotten in trouble if I had wanted to. Those other eyes would say, "I know your mother." And that would be the threat. My friends and I went to a party one night. My mother knew everything that occurred before I got home. She told me about some things that took place that I did not know about. I only found out on Monday when we all got back to school. The funny thing about it is that this was before cell phones. Before social media. This was even before cordless phones. She knew what was going on.

Be active like she was with us. Know the friends of the people in your care. Know what they are like. If anything were to happen, you would know where to look and what to do because you know them so well. I know about many that keep tabs on their family. They will make sure that everyone is where they are supposed to be when they are supposed to be in place. Validate everyone. It may not seem like it, but this will prevent some of the wrong things from happening. Validate the schools. Validate the environment in which everyone will be spending time. Validate the church to be the right one. Validate everything. You may ask, "How do I validate?" This is part of the relationship with God. Check things out with God in prayer. Do not just request and request and request. You must be quiet and listen. See what He has to say. (It will always be in line with His Word.) Check to see if this is the right school. Is this the place we are to live? Are these the right people to be around? Are we doing the right things that He would have for us to do?

> **Do not be deceived: "Evil company corrupts good habits." 1 Corinthians 15:33**

Future generations can be influenced by what we allow. As it is said, God will allow the things that you allow. He put that accountability and responsibility in your hands. We cannot put this off on others. Be the gatekeeper. Be that watchman on the wall. You cannot be caught sleeping on the job. Do not fall asleep at the wheel. As much as I would hate to say it, there are many that are asleep. They become distracted or have too much on their plate to address the things that should be a priority.

POSITION YOURSELF

Position yourself and your family to have the right influences in your lives. One of the best suggestions I would have would be a good church. That's not to say that every church is perfect, but being in a good church would be a place to position yourself. You can grow and develop in different areas of your life.

According to the Institute of Family Studies, the average American congregation is roughly 61% female and 39% male. Five out of six men claim to be Christian. Only a portion of them attend church on a regular basis. Growing up, my dad would be at home and not come to church. Looking back on things, I can see now how there was a difference when he got baptized and started going to church. He was involved, and things were changing for the better in his life, which impacted us. As a child, I could no longer go to the bathroom to waste time during a church service. He made sure I was in my seat. He gave tithes, and I saw things turn for the better in that area. I remember riding in the car with him in the passenger seat on the way to a Bible study that he was encouraged to attend. To my amazement, he recited a whole chapter while he was driving. I was following every word in the Bible as he quoted the chapter. Some things that God has done we are not able to explain. The understanding would come from God's Word. Attending church can give you the wisdom from God that a Master's degree would not be able to provide. What you put into it is what you get out of going to church. You can grow and develop in different areas of your life. Making good decisions would help you to position yourself also. The Word of God would be a guide to position yourself to be a good gatekeeper.

Making good decisions would help you to position yourself. Having the wrong friends, bad company, and doing the wrong things will not help you get into the right position. It would draw you away from it.

SET THE EXAMPLE

Whether we realize it or not, we are teaching and being an example. The reason is that we are being watched. Others will do what they see you do. You may not have signed up for that role, but you are sometimes in that role, like it or not. I can think of the things and people I watched as a child. You pick up things and develop habits so naturally. We should all be the right example for others to see. If others are to pick up habits from us, they need to be the right ones to carry on to others. As I said before, if you cannot find a good example to follow, you can be the example yourself. You don't have to wait on one.

One important factor is how women are treated. Do not allow the movies of the streets to teach how a woman is to be treated. Work to stay consistent with treating her the right way. In order to keep chivalry alive, we must implement this with those that are in our care and do it as an example for them to follow. To keep things balanced and not allow others to take advantage or distract you.

> **Husbands, likewise, dwell with them with understanding, giving honor to the wife, as to the weaker vessel, and as being heirs together of the grace**

of life, that your prayers may not be hindered. 1 Peter 3:7

There are benefits to treating the woman the way that she was intended to be treated. This is why we open doors. Walk against the traffic and let her walk away from the traffic while placing her on the side to be protected. This is not to say that she is weak, but we have to treat a woman the way that has been outlined for us to treat her as the weaker vessel. This does not imply that women are weak. We are to treat them as if they are the weaker vessel with the care that we provide for them by being a gentleman.

Husbands, love your wives, just as Christ also loved the church and gave Himself for her... Ephesians 5:25

When we can see things from God's perspective, it can help us to know the right way to treat others. It may not be how someone specifically wants to be treated, but we are to treat others according to God's Word.

WRAP UP

Everything that glitters is not gold. Things can appear to be the right thing when they come to you. We have to validate the things that we encounter. Will need to be watchful and inspect the fruit. Jesus said, "You will know them by their fruit." Know those that labor among you. Know the things that make up your environment. You do not have to only be a gatekeeper. You can also look for ways to have a positive impact on all the things that are in your care. A watchman not only protects but also impacts.

FINAL WRAP UP

You do not have to be limited to what the world says you can be. You can do what God's Word says you can do. You can be what God's Word says you can be. You do not have to be labeled by others. Find your gifts and talents to be successful in God's eyes. Not what others call success or what others may want you to be. You were created in His image and His likeness. Not theirs. Be the person God created you to be. There is only one you. Please don't sell us short of what God has put in you to bring to the table.

An invitation has been provided at the beginning of this letter. By taking steps to invite Jesus into your heart, you will have a better understanding of the topics discussed in this letter. I pray that if you have not taken the steps, you do so now.

If you have gotten away from God in the past, I encourage you to recommit your life to Him again. It would be a great thing for you and give you understanding as you read the content of this letter. There is no judgment here. I'm only helping to get your spiritual needs met.

Give your life to Christ.

> "...for all have sinned and fall short of the glory of God." Romans 3:23

> "...if you confess with your mouth the Lord Jesus and believe in your heart that God has raised Him from the dead, you will be saved. For with the heart one believes unto righteousness, and with the mouth confession is made unto salvation." Romans 10:9-10

This can be done in prayer. Invite Jesus Christ into your heart.

Believe that He is the son of God and that God has raised Him from the dead. Confess Jesus Christ as Lord. Receive Him as Lord.

SAY THIS PRAYER:

I am a sinner; I need a savior. I need Jesus. I turn from sin, and I turn to You. I believe in my heart that You raised Jesus from the dead, and I ask Jesus now to come into my heart and be the Lord of my life. I receive Him now as Lord of my life, and I confess with my mouth that Jesus is Lord! Thank you for my salvation! In Jesus' name, Amen.

Now, according to Scripture, you will have a better understanding of God's Word.

> **And He said, "To you it has been given to know the mysteries of the kingdom of God, but to the rest it is given in parables, that 'Seeing they may not see, And hearing they may not understand.' Luke 8:10**

Rededicate your life back to God.

> "If we confess our sins, He is faithful and just to forgive us our sins and to cleanse us from all unrighteousness." 1 John 1:9

> "As far as the east is from the west, So far has He removed our transgressions from us." Psalm 103:12

SAY THIS PRAYER:

Father, I have sinned, and I ask you to forgive me. I turn away from sin, and I receive your forgiveness. I forgive myself. Now, I recommit my life to you afresh. I break the power of the devil over my life, in Jesus' name. Thank you, Father, for receiving me again and allowing me to have a right standing with You. I confess that all my sins and transgressions have been removed.

RESOURCES

1. Brennan Center for Justice Website
2. https://www.brennancenter.org/our-work/research-reports/myths-and-realities-understanding-recent-trends-violent-crime?ms=gad_crime%20statistics_617000456634_8626214133_143843260761&gclid=CjoKCQjwt_qgBhDFARIsABcDjOfJgNKPsE30VPNs4GnPa8_obJewoK44ga-C-8R6DvJ9o32UrRvBABAaAvviEALw_wcB
3. **Source:** FBI Uniform Crime Reporting Program, Crime in the United States, 2020, Table 1A.
4. Men in the Church
5. https://www.capterra.com/resources/where-are-all-the-men-exploring-the-gender-gap-in-church/
6. To My Sisters In Christ

ABOUT THE AUTHOR

A native of Charlotte North Carolina. Born the youngest of three children Crawford grew up on the west side Charlotte. Even as westside resident Crawford attended schools in different parts of the city of Charlotte. He never wanted to live life through traditions or conforming to a mold that others would try to set him out to complete. Never remained on a path just because it was the popular route to take. Brought up in a Baptist church and did not develop a relationship with Christ until after high school. Did not develop a true relationship with God until he was off on his own away from home. The journey with Christ went from carnality to authentic with lessons learned along with the mentors, teachers and others that God has led to be part of his life. Works with different organizations to help win others to Christ. Crawford continues to serve in the helps ministry to serve others from different walks of life.

www.ingramcontent.com/pod-product-compliance
Lightning Source LLC
LaVergne TN
LVHW061038070526
838201LV00073B/5094